Seth has lived these words, fought for them, wrestled lies to the ground, and found love on the other side. May we slow down, pay attention, and wake up to the freedom we've been craving all along.

—REBEKAH LYONS, bestselling author,
Rhythms of Renewal and *You Are Free*

The Book of Waking Up truly is for all of us. In these pages you will not find the dreaded alarm clock, no. This is a glorious song of joy, of honesty, and of wonder-working power. These lyrical, honest, humble words will open eyes, unclench fists, and cause souls to rise up in love.

—SARAH BESSEY, author, *Miracles and Other
Reasonable Things* and *Jesus Feminist*

Seth cheerfully challenges the lies all addicts tell themselves to get them through the night, because he knows, by experience, that the truth will set you free. Whether or not you think you're an addict, read this book and learn.

—BISHOP GREG BREWER, Bishop of the
Episcopal Diocese of Central Florida

Sobriety is complicated. No one has it all figured out, but no one writes toward it and speaks toward it and leads me toward it like Seth Haines. His writing is a map and a comfort. A lamp and a warm hearth. I trust his words in my joy and in my pain.

—ANNIE F. DOWNS, bestselling author,
100 Days to Brave and *Remember God*

Combining prose with poetry, theology with biography, and rapture born of rupture, Seth paves the way for those of us who, having grown tired of our wandering and wavering affections, are trying to figure out how to get back home. I can't recommend this book to you highly enough.

—SCOTT SAULS, senior pastor, Christ Presbyterian
Church; author, *Jesus Outside the Lines* and *Irresistible Faith*

Years ago, Gerald May's theologically rich and psychologically trust-worthy *Addiction and Grace* became my go-to resource. Today it's *The Book of Waking Up*. I'm so grateful to Seth for his wisdom and vulnerability in it.

—CHUCK DEGROAT, professor of pastoral care and
Christian spirituality, Western Theological Seminary

Seth Haines does two things in this book: he awakens us to our addic-tions and reveals himself as a thoughtful, incisive, and skilled writer. This book invites us to dive deep into the condition of our hearts, and offers guidance, hope, and direction for a better way.

—MIKE COSPER, author, *Recapturing the Wonder* and
Rhythms of Grace; founder, Harbor Media

This book encourages us not merely to wake up from addiction but also to wake up to adoration of the God who loves us and promises to be faithful to us forever. It is most effective when read slowly, reflecting on the challenges offered and allowing God to transform us.

—GLENN R. KREIDER, professor of theological studies, Dallas
Theological Seminary; editor-in-chief, *Bibliotheca Sacra*

THE BOOK OF WAKING UP

ALSO BY SETH HAINES

Coming Clean: A Story of Faith

THE BOOK OF WAKING UP

*experiencing the divine
love that reorders a life*

SETH HAINES

ZONDERVAN®

ZONDERVAN

The Book of Waking Up
Copyright © 2020 by Seth Haines

Requests for information should be addressed to:
Zondervan, *3900 Sparks Dr. SE, Grand Rapids, Michigan 49546*

Zondervan titles may be purchased in bulk for educational, business, fundraising, or promotional use. For information, please email SpecialMarkets@Zondervan.com.

ISBN 978-0-310-35396-6 (softcover)

ISBN 978-0-310-35859-6 (audio)

ISBN 978-0-310-35398-0 (ebook)

Cover design: Curt Diepenhorst
Cover illustrations: Thoom / Forgem / Shutterstock
Interior design: Denise Froehlich

Printed in the United States of America

19 20 21 22 23   LSC   10 9 8 7 6 5 4 3 2 1

In his book *For the Life of the World*, Alexander Schmemann writes, "The purpose of this book is a humble one. It is to remind its readers that in Christ, life—life in all its totality—was returned to man, given again as sacrament and communion, made Eucharist." I could only hope to scratch the surface of the depth found in Schmemann's little book on the sacramental life. Still, this simple emotional apologetic tugs some of the same strings, I hope. So if you take nothing else from this work, may it be Schmemann's reminder that life (all of it) has been returned to you as sacrament and communion. Follow these bread crumbs till the end. Eat those bread crumbs. Drink the wine too.

Contents

FOREWORD

Seth Haines has been one of my favorite faith writers since the moment I finished his first book, *Coming Clean,* so I've been waiting for this book with great anticipation. Seth sent me an early manuscript as a gift with no request attached. He offered me these pages because he thought they might be good company in the darkness that has marked my life in recent years, and indeed they have been, profoundly so.

Seth is a Southern storyteller, very much at home in that rich communion of poets and writers who don't flinch in the face of darkness, are at home in the natural world, and aren't afraid of a little mystery. And he's a really good question-asker—for what it's worth, the people I trust most these days are the question people, not the answer people.

The way of being Christian that Seth articulates is one that resonates with me so deeply. It's a rigorous discipleship, one that requires excavation and honesty and the shedding of long-held attachments, but it's also a gentle discipleship, rooted in Divine Love and offering the connection that we've been searching for in so many of our addictions and dead ends.

We live in a culture obsessed with both image management and pain management, and this book is a hundred and sixty-three elegant and honest invitations to stop managing and start living. Seth has a way of touching a bruise that you've been trying to protect, but he does it with compassion and empathy, inviting you to tell the truth about your pain because he has gone first, telling the truth about his. What a gift!

In this midlife, change-riddled, loss-heavy season of my life, I'm getting pretty comfortable with walking alone, largely because I find those too-bright and too-happy voices so much more offensive than silence to my ears these days. But God has, in his goodness, sent a few voices my way, voices saturated with honesty, tinged with pain, singing in low tones that keep me good company along the way, and Seth's voice in these pages has been one of the most trustworthy. I'm so grateful.

—SHAUNA NIEQUIST

Acknowledgments

Acknowledgments are frightening, a reminder that both my memory and imagination are fracturing. This much is certain: I'll forget someone who sparked some thought that made its way into this book. Please accept my apologies at the outset.

Amber: We have risked and rioted, shaken fists and beds, and fallen together in both elation and emptiness. Even in this falling, though, we've fallen down together. We've risen together too. I suppose that's what marriage means, committing to the deep magic of love, whether falling or rising. I'm glad we're in the deep magic together.

Stephanie Smith: You know the fights to pick, the fights to avoid (particularly the ones I pick with myself), and the ways words can be honed to the point of art. You are more than an editor. You are my friend.

Zondervan team: This was a difficult work, but your faith, patience, and commitment in and to it helped me pull it across the finish line. Thank you. (And Brian Phipps, your attention to detail is nothing short of inspired. Special thanks to you.)

Whitney Gossett: I invited you along for this ride, and

when I found myself road weary, you took the wheel. I think it's a broader metaphor for something. Every insufferable writer needs a partner, consultant, business dreamer, and friend who can suffer him. Thanks for putting up with me.

John Blase: You have taught me how to incarnate, how to take, eat, and drink the Stuff of Earth. You are Common Tribe.

Winn Collier: You undercut my identity when I needed it most, stripped the scarlet A of *alcoholic* from my conscience. It was the Genesis of everything in these pages.

To the Kindred Collective: You were the crew I didn't know I needed. Some combination of you and Kentucky drizzle made me believe again. All things are possible.

John Ray: You are proof of the spiritual acuity that comes only through pain. Thank you for not quitting.

Mike and Corrie Rusch: You facilitated the evening of my sacramental awakening. The bread. The wine. Thank you; I will love you to the end.

Felicia and Alex: You fueled this work with caffeine, presence, and conversation. The season we shared at Puritan Uptown has marked me. I hope it has marked you.

Masie Cochran: You are the black to my white, the perfect foil to my unbridled optimism, and a carrier of guarded hope. Conversations with you helped me see this work in a new light.

Dan Johnson: You led me through an Ignatian journey, unlocked the ways of thinking about things as a saint might. I haven't quite figured it all out yet, but I suppose that's what a lifetime is for. Thank you.

Bob Shari: You were once advocates, then sounding boards, and now friends. I'm grateful one set of notorious sinners found another.

Sammers, Gagnons, Masons: What does it mean to live in a Community of Waking? I'm still learning. Thanks for learning along with the Haines people.

Steve Wiens, Kevin Cawley, Scott Sauls: Each of you provided some piece to this puzzle. Though I find myself trending Catholic, I'd embed myself in your respective communities of waking any day. As a set, you represent the best of the pastorate.

Shauna Niequist: In this world of social climbing, power bartering, and the commoditization of creativity, you stand apart. I've always been grateful for that. Thank you for penning the foreword for this work. You were always my first choice.

Mom and Dad: Thanks for not being afraid of the Catholic church. It likely saved my faith.

Thanks to all those who helped fuel this work on Patreon, especially those of you in the Publisher tiers: Erika Morrison (peace, sister); Rachel "Marshy B" Dockery; Rebecca Wimer; Rachel Hagstrom; Lanelle King; Roslyn Bourgeois; William Ogles; Dorothy Camak; Darin Shrock; Julie Cannon; Elizabeth Marshall; Sarah Rosangela; Becky McCoy; Bridgette Templeton; Annie Parsons; Janna Barber; Troy McLaughlin; Noel Young; Mary Byam-Smith; Beth Siegel; Linda Hopson; Peggy Miller; Ron Lambert; Claude Dickson; Janet Chastain; Ron Rogers; Marjorie Budrow; Karoletha Stone; and Ron Anderson.

Honorable Mention: Special thanks to Jonathan Merritt, who has forever soiled the phrase "undrunk."

BEFORE THE QUESTIONS BEGIN

I wake to sleep, and take my waking slow.

—THEODORE ROETHKE, "THE WAKING"

1. The Way We Start a New Day: An Introduction

In the comfort of my bed, I dreamed the pleasant dreams of childhood. On occasion, I'd fly, which felt more akin to being flown like a kite, wind pressing up against my torso. I'd rise above the summer-crisped cow fields of central Texas or the moss-spotted, blue-gray Ozark-stone riverbeds. These floating dreams were ozone-laced apparitions in which, for the most part, I stayed tethered fifty feet above the ground, the limit of my childhood imagination. On occasion, though, my wings carried me past the tops of houses, trees, and sometimes mountains. I'd float upward through clouds and almost into orbit. I'd float and float, numb to the prospect of falling until a fit of shaking set in. In that turbulence, I'd fall a few feet, then a few more. My bones would rattle and I'd flail my arms trying to stay afloat. In those dreams turned nightmares, dread set in.

The icicles pumping from my heart and into my limbs, my arms, my legs—those are my earliest childhood memories of fear. It was a fear both hollow and lead filled. It was the sweaty, muted dread of falling from the heights of my own imagination. And how far down was the floor?

That childhood dream was a recurring one, and I do not recall whether I ever fell to my death. Here's what I do recall, though: on more than one occasion, while tethered to that anchor of fear pulling me earthward, I heard a song. It was distant at first, like the tinkling of a music box in the clouds. Then, with more clarity, it came like the tune of a neighborhood ice-cream truck. The volume of that song rose and words came in a slow soprano, lifting me back through the clouds, pulling me into the deepening gray of space, then into the liminal black behind my eyelids. As I opened my eyes to gathering light, as the contours of my bedroom came into focus, there was my mother, standing above my bed and singing.

Good morning to you. Good morning to you.
We're all in our places with sunshiny faces.
This is the way we start a new day.

My mother sang this song with her face shining. This was the way all her wake-up songs started—in the key of joy.

The beginning of my sober years felt much like waking up to my mother's song. It was a slow waking from some dreamy death spiral. And as I've talked to others who are in recovery from their own coping mechanisms, they've said the same thing.

So often, sobriety comes like an unexpected sweet song.

2. Waking from Addiction, Waking to Adoration

There are things I'd like you to know about this book.

First, though it builds on many of the lessons I learned in my sobriety journey, this book is not so much about addiction or dependency or even sobriety. It's about waking. And when I say waking, I mean both waking from and waking to. Waking from the numb floating, the drifting higher and higher. Waking from your attempts to self-soothe, to anesthetize your pain. Waking from the false, the fake, the pleasant dream turned crystalline fear that always precedes the crash. Waking from dependency, addiction, recurring habits that might do you in.

Waking from your addictions—this is only a part of what it means to wake up. What do you wake to? This is the other part.

Waking from addiction and to the transcendent, the numinous, the cosmic, quantum healer. Waking from addiction and to the Divine Love of God expressed through Jesus, the Christ who wants to repair every frayed nerve, every broken synapse, every jacked-up desire. (This we'll call the Divine Love throughout this book.)[1] As you wake to the Divine Love, fix your eyes on it. Root into it. Adore it.

How do I wake from addiction and to adoration?

That's the subject of this book.

---

1 This usage, "Divine Love," is not some nonspecific hippy-dippy way of describing the love of God in Christ. Instead, it's a usage found in the writings of great saints. Section 160 is an example of St. Francis de Sales' use of the term.

3. What's in a Word? "Coping Mechanisms"

In this book, we'll explore words and their meanings. Among those words, we'll examine the term *addiction*. As you read, I hope you'll see how anything can form a sort of slavish attachment, a sort of addiction.

Habits like checking Twitter, Instagram, or Facebook? Yes.

Substances like booze and opioids? Of course.

Dependencies on the material, on money, on entertainment, on sex? No doubt.

I'll suggest that our bad habits, addictions, and dependencies are the things we use, attach to, or love in an effort to cope with the pains of life. So throughout this book, when you see the term *coping mechanism,* read it as my shorthand for any habit, addiction, or dependency.

Coping mechanisms—we all have them, even the best of us. Mine was booze, then book buying, then a bowl of cereal and a good Netflix binge. Anything to take my mind off the pain. Some might overeat or undereat or exercise too much or binge shop or click-click-click on porn into the wee hours of the morning.

Biblical characters had their slavish attachments too, characters like Paul the apostle and Jesus' best friend, Peter. It should come as no surprise that having experienced the Divine Love that woke them from their slumber, they used waking language in their letter-writing campaigns.

4. Wake Up, Paul!

There was a man named Jesus, the great God with Us, and this was his call: "What I say to you I say to all: Stay awake" (Mark 13:37 ESV).

That great God with Us met a Christian-killer, a real pious prig named Saul, on the road to Damascus. He knocked that prig off his high horse and locked him in the blackness of blindness. Jesus met him in that darkness, woke him to a new life eventually marked by a new name—Paul. He showed Paul the way his coping mechanisms had led him into a great sleep. What coping mechanisms? The dependency on self-righteous priggery, on doing all the right things, on his pious cause—the genocide of Christ's followers.

Paul also woke into a new, sober way of living, the way of living into Christ's love. It should be no surprise that Paul penned these words, then: "Awake, O sleeper, and arise from the dead, and Christ will shine on you" (Eph. 5:14 ESV). He put it this way too: "So then let us not sleep, as others do [as I had], but let us keep awake and be sober" (1 Thess. 5:6 ESV).

5. WAKE UP, PETER!

Peter, a man whose anxiety got the best of him, who denied Jesus to save his skin on Good Friday morning, woke into a new way of being too. After the resurrection, after Jesus did exactly what he promised, Christ came and shook Peter out of his self-loathing, his self-preservation, his self-soothing and invited the disciple into Divine Love. Relationship restored, Jesus gave Peter a grand charge: lead my church.

Awakened to God's love and motivated by Christ's call, Peter steered the people of God to walk in true sobriety. In his letter to the church, he writes, "[Cast] all your anxieties on him, because he cares for you. Be sober-minded; be watchful" (1 Peter 5:7–8 ESV). Sober and watchful—what does it mean? To Peter, it means casting our anxieties on the Divine Love instead of medicating them with our own coping mechanisms.

6. Wake Up, Everyone Else!

As if to make himself clear, the great God with Us visited his beloved friend John in a revelatory apocalyptic vision, a vision induced by neither shroom nor LSD. In that vision, John saw his resurrected friend, Jesus, who spoke a waking word: "I am coming like a thief! Blessed is the one who *stays awake,* keeping his garments on, that he may not go about naked and be seen exposed!" (Rev. 16:15 ESV, emphasis added). Through John, Jesus reminded his people to stay awake, to stay ready, to stay sober, to stay clothed in his love so we wouldn't be found showing our hindquarters when Christ comes calling. And even if we don't live to see some apocalyptic return, we each have our own end of days to reckon with. How silly to be found in the arms of lesser loves when that day comes.

7. A Full Refund, Maybe

Jesus' friends understood his call—stay sober, stay awake, remain watchful—and so they gave it to us straight. They knew the truth: dream-drifting in coping mechanisms keeps us from experiencing the nonanxious love of God. Maybe you know this to be true. Maybe not. And maybe you live in such a self-actualized state of wakefulness that you live addiction free, free of chemical, emotional, or material dependence. Congratulations. This book is not for you. Please contact me for a refund.[2]

If you're still reading, here is the second thing I'd like you to know about this book: this wake-up song—"Good Morning to You"—is not just for the fall-down alcoholics, the heroin addicts, or the rehab bound. In my experience, those we're quick to label addicts are just like the rest of us, only with an acute awareness of their addictions, their propensity to use drugs to lull themselves to sleep to the pains of life. They know the limits of their willpower, the ways their best intentions break. There are plenty of books written for them. (I know. I've been the target audience.)

This book is not only for those with classic addictions but also for those who use more socially acceptable coping mechanisms: workaholics, compulsive shoppers, executives addicted to peer approval, and yes, even compulsive TwInstaBook scrollers. We've all found ourselves asleep at one point or another, and most of us will feel the tug of that slumber again. This forms the basis of the

---

2   Offer contingent upon the following: proof of purchase, proof of proper attachment as later defined in this book, corroborating affidavits by three relatives living in your home or other close friends who have insight into your freedom from chemical, emotional, or material attachments, addictions, or dependencies.

working hypothesis of this book: we're all addicted (or attached) to something. We all use some kind of coping mechanism.

In other words, if you have a pulse, you have a problem.

In other words, we're all in this together.

8. Addiction Exhibits

For reference, and as anecdotal evidence supporting my hypothesis that we're all addicted to something, consider exhibits A through E:

Exhibit A: In 2013 I quit the bottle. I kept a journal over the first ninety days of sobriety, a journal which became my book, *Coming Clean: A Story of Faith*. In *Coming Clean*, I shared how the near death of my son exposed my belief that the God I worship was unable to hear or heal, that he was absent at best or nonexistent at worst. I learned that pain was more than soul pain. It burned, bled, felt as real as any gunshot to the stomach. I followed that pain into a decision I'd made to numb myself. How else can you cope when life's every edge is ragged pain? So I chose to sleepwalk through my life, Gordon's gin my medicine.

I spun yarns in those sleepy drunk years: "I can quit whenever I want. I don't have a real problem. I've never hit my wife, lost my job, or gotten a DWI, so I can't be alcohol dependent." I was asleep, convinced as I was to the contrary.

In *Coming Clean*, I shared how the God of healing found me, a wounded boy sleeping. He didn't come promising the healing of my son or the poetic end of all my existential pain. He didn't come in that sky-blue VW bus offering feel-good medicine either, though that would have been an awesome trip. Instead, he came singing songs of comfort.

Good morning to you. Good morning to you.

He found me over those ninety days, day after day, and woke me into something a little less broken, a little less attached to the bottle, a little more attached to him.

This is the way we start a new day.

I wrote this story of faith, shared it with the world, then I hit the road. I spoke to folks who had their own soul pain, who confessed their own years of sleepiness. Consider them exhibits B through E.

Exhibit B: She'd always measured a pound more than her father's image of perfect, she said. She'd been bulimic these last fifteen years. Through the binge and the purge, through the euphoria that came from bowing to the porcelain god, she'd numbed herself to the pain of living up to her father's *Playboy* ideal. That is, until she looked in the mirror again. She was a pillar of the church, a pastor's wife. Even still, she chose sleep.

Exhibit C: A Midwestern soccer mom felt trapped in her Yukon. She was always carting her kids around while her workaholic husband spat on her dreams of vocation. She loved her Percocet, the way it helped her float above all the go-go-go, all those droning PTA meetings.

Exhibit D: A Southern preacher was afraid of failure, always worried about letting his people down. Acid ate a hole in his stomach in the wee hours of the morning, but the nip of whiskey and sleeping pills helped him push into dreams. Tell the elders? No way, he said. He was living a life of fireable offenses.

Exhibit E: The accountant in Middle America grew up in the scarcity of dirt-floor poverty. He was a compulsive shopper. Click, click, click—there wasn't any category of thing he hadn't one-clicked into his mailbox over the last year. Except a car. He'd had that internet purchase delivered from Florida on a flatbed truck. Why was there never enough?

9. A GRIM TRUTH

We are people of coping mechanisms ranging from the illegal to the socially acceptable. No matter the substance, material, vice, or habit, we all use them to numb ourselves to pain. And even in my days of "sobriety" (quotes intended) I found a grim truth: I'm still so prone to numbing myself to sleep in new ways. Increasing internet usage, social media consumption, vocation, occupation, one-click purchasing—aren't these just permutations of my need to overdo anything? Aren't I becoming compulsive in my need to be entertained or distracted? Why, in all my "sobriety," do I so often feel less than sober?

This, I think, gets to the guts of it. If we're all drunk on something, if we're all asleep or pulled toward the tendency of sleep, how do we wake into a true, lasting, joyful sobriety that does not give way to a different sort of slumber?[3]

This book, I hope, will help us answer that question.

---

3   I once heard a sex addict use "we're all addicted to something" in a way that minimized his addiction. Sure, he was addicted to the sexual exploitation of women, but it wasn't any worse than so-and-so's shopping addiction. Pointing to the addiction of others in an attempt to minimize your own addiction is simply blame shifting and misses the point.

10. The Waking Library

There is a big-box bookstore in Fayetteville containing row upon row of self-help books, and last Saturday, I hopped from the fiction section to the self-help section to scan the covers. The titles were big and blocky, and almost without exception, the authors' faces were stamped on the front. Each author was white, their hair well coiffed, their teeth straight as piano keys. Smiling, they offered the following kind of help (more or less, with some slight titling revisions):

> *The Wednesday Way to Winning Marriage: Orgasmacizing*
> *Your Sex Life on Hump Day*
> *Quit It: Training Yourself in the Art of Stopping Stuff*
> *How to Find Money, Power, and Fame: How I*
> *Achieved What You Desperately Want*

The topics ran the gamut, but sequestered on two shelves were the self-help books on addiction. (It is worth mentioning that these titles and covers were more self-effacing and less marked by the faces of success.) All these books written by all these authors, most of whom had faced and overcome their demons.

I scanned the books. Books on alcoholism, drug addiction, sex addiction. Books with the words *recovery* and *steps* and *overcoming* in the title. There was a book on overcoming addiction through meditation. So many books. Why hadn't I read any of them? Had I avoided them because they were tucked away with the well-manicured, ever-smiling, quite-fashionable gurus? Had I value-judged these sorts of books?

Sure, I've read books on addiction, books that helped me understand my shaking insobriety, but they weren't self-help books. I devoured Mary Karr's *Lit*, and I loved *In the Realm of Hungry Ghosts*, Gabor Maté's stunning exploration of human being and addiction.

I read Bill Clegg's *Portrait of an Addict as a Young Man,* Elizabeth Vargas's *Between Breaths,* and Thomas De Quincey's *Confessions of an English Opium-Eater.* I love those books because they don't offer easy answers to human angst. What's more, the authors show what I've experienced to be at the root of all addiction—pain.

So know this about this book: it is not a self-help book. I wouldn't categorize those addiction books tucked away in the self-help section of Big-Box Books "R" Us that way either.

If I were allowed a stint as a bookstore manager, I'd create a new category for those books: Books of Waking Up. I'd load the section with those more self-helpy addiction titles, but I'd also scatter in some Karr and Maté and Vargas too. I'd throw in some De Quincey, Russell Brand, and Gerald May for good measure. I'd include books about the body, about neurochemistry, and the confluence of pain and addiction. And if you visited my store, I'd lead you straight to that library of waking and ask you to pick your poison—or antivenom, as it were. I'd invite you to read it all, to soak it up, to understand. And then, I'd invite you to press into a more lasting experience.

This book? It is that library.

11. The Layout

The last thing I'd like you to know about this book: it's a snowball rolling downhill, a building argument, a series of smaller parts of a much bigger whole. I've done my best to organize it that way. It's meant to be picked up, read, put down, and reflected on. More than anything, it's meant to lead you somewhere.

As you read, you'll find each major section begins with a question:

What is the problem?
What is the pain?
What is addiction, really?
What is sobriety?
How do we wake to the sober way?

Following these section questions is a series of numbered reflections, examples, stories, and supporting evidence. These subsections build on each other and attempt some resolution of the section question. The answers to these section questions, when taken together, are meant to comprise a singular argument: there is a way to live in the wakefulness of true inner sobriety, and it begins with proper attachment to Christ, the Divine Love, the first light of the morning.

12. I AIN'T YOUR GURU

Finally, there is no small amount of time, talent, and effort put into the practice of guruism these days. People have questions. Gurus have answers. Answers are marketable.

If there's one thing I'm not setting out to be, it's a guru on pain, addiction, sobriety, or anything, really. If I am anything, it's the following, in no particular order:

- A screwup.
- A fella of faith (and doubt) who knows what it's like to be asleep to anything divine.
- A nerd who's spent countless hours trying to sort out his human experience—the experience of pain, addiction, and ultimately, healing—and who's tried to find the universal threads of that story.
- A layman with enough biblical knowledge to see the parallels in his life to the lives of folks like David (the sex addict), Jacob (the greedy), and maybe even Judas (the suicidal betrayer).
- A father who'd like to keep his kids from the same goo that mired their old man. (Is such a thing possible?)
- An alarm clock.
- A wakeup call.
- On a good day, the personification of reveille.

If you're looking for a guru, there is no shortage of folks who'll take your money to fill that niche. But if you're looking for a new way to rise and shine, a multilayered wake-up song, come along. Let's walk into wakefulness together.

What Is the Problem?

*It is funny how mortals always picture us as
putting things into their minds: in reality our
best work is done by keeping things out.*

—C. S. Lewis, *The Screwtape Letters*

13. SOLVING THE APOCALYPSE

In a 1995 edition of *The Orange County Register,* a professor at McMaster University in Ontario described famed physicist Albert Einstein's approach to solving the apocalypse: "When Einstein was asked how he would save the world in one hour, he said he'd spend fifty-five minutes defining the problem and five minutes solving it."

It was an apocryphal quote, one which Einstein likely didn't speak. But still, isn't there wisdom buried there? When we examine our habits, addictions, dependencies, and vices, we so often ask this question: Why can't we just quit?

The alcoholic asks it this way: Why can't I stop drinking?

The workaholic, porn addict, or shopaholic asks it another: Why can't I shut off the computer?

The runaholic (yes, this is a thing) asks, Why do I keep trying to outpace my problems?

The approvaholic (yes, this is a thing too) asks, Why can't I say no to the next PTA assignment, organizing the next church potluck, and hosting the next neighborhood party, all of which fall in the same week?

How to quit—this is the solution, not the problem. But to reach the solution, we have to define the problem.

What is the problem underlying our coping mechanisms?

They *do* something for us.

14. MANAGING DEMONS

He had a problem, and he was getting to the point where he knew it.

He was bipolar, he said, and he'd been haunted by clownish mania and suicidal depression his entire life. One day was a fit a minute, an idea a second, and the next day existential Ecclesiastical depression anchored him to the bed. ("Vanity of vanities; all is vanity," he was fond of saying.) A church-planter, a man with mega-church aspirations, he'd come to the end of his rope years ago. At the end of that rope, thick in his haunting, he turned to self-medication.

"In fits of mania," he said, "the booze slows me down. In bouts of depression, it numbs the weight of the world, all the meaningless-ness of everything. You know?"

Do I know?

"Have you talked to your wife? A therapist? Your church folks?" I asked. He gave the answer I expected, the consistent, near-certain, ever-human universal answer.

"No. No one knows. Not really," he said. Then, index fingers pointing at his noggin in a swirling motion, he asked, "And even if I quit, how would I manage all of this?"

I've heard this story too many times to count over the last few years, a story told by pastors, housewives, and inmates alike. The thing underlying so many of our habits, addictions, dependencies, or vices is different: mental illness, abuse, disease, rejection, the pangs of hunger. The numbing agents are different too: booze, overeating, overworking, shopping, binging and purging. In almost every case, though, there's a common human element. Aren't so many of us using something to manage "all of this"? Don't we all hope to hide our crazy under a bushel?

Yes, I think.

15. Needling Words

Manage, manage, manage—even I try to manage what the pastor called "all of this."

Outside of the Sunday communion wine and that time I took a luxurious swig of my wife's pomegranate juice and vodka (believing it to be my pomegranate juice and water), I laid off the sauce for three solid years. On that long, dry, dry, dry road, I learned something about "all of this": there are times when the brain plays tricks on you, when it speaks a needling word of desire.

Some time ago, I had one of those days when the needling wouldn't stop. My second thoughts about sobriety occupied most of my afternoon. Those second thoughts became third, fourth, and fifth thoughts as the day's stresses multiplied. There was a less than favorable family medical update, and I second-guessed my abstinence. The office finance department called, said I had a client with an overdue account and asked if I'd try to collect it. That's when I third-guessed my personal temperance movement. A good and proper marital spat rounded out my workday, and who could blame me for fourth-guessing sobriety after a quality lovers' quarrel?

I was anxious, felt helpless, incompetent, and misunderstood. That's when the needling words came, the compulsion, and it came laced with the smell of gin and whiskey.

What could one nip hurt?

It's good medicine, easy medicine too.

Eat, drink, and be merry, and if not merry, at least numb.

The needling words burrowed past my inner ear, triggered the nostalgia of gin's juniper and the oak barrels of my favorite bourbon. Call it a flashback, a haunting, an overactive olfactory system. Call it crazy. Call it whatever you want. The truth is, on that day I couldn't shake the smells.

In the evening, nerves on fire, I wanted rid of the needling words. I dusted off the old standby prayer that carried me through my earliest days of sobriety—*Lord Jesus Christ, Son of God, have mercy on me, a sinner*—and pushed through the back door, making my way to the folding love seat by a one-acre pond. I reached into the garbage can beside that love seat and grabbed a handful of fish pellets, which I tossed to the water's edge, just beyond the shade of the red cedar. The water bubbled as the catfish exercised their animal instincts, their insatiable appetites, their inability to say no to stinky pellets. I watched those fish, and I prayed the Jesus Prayer again and again.

Lord Jesus Christ, Son of God, have mercy on me, a sinner.
Lord Jesus Christ, Son of God, have mercy on me, a sinner.
Lord Jesus Christ, Son of God, have mercy on me, a sinner.

Somehow, that prayer, the fish, the wind on the water—all of it—hushed those needling words. Somehow, the crazy anxiety dissipated. Somehow, my compulsions dissolved.

In a new calm, I waded into my own mud. What was underneath the want to drink? What was underneath the anxiety? Why did a fit of everyday anxiety bring back so many memories of the boozy days, the days I was unsober? And why didn't those same compulsions needle their way into my noggin on those occasions when I partook of full-bodied communion wine? How was it that the Eucharist undid my compulsions?

Days later, I texted a friend and outed my thirst for liquor. (This practice of outing, it tethers me to saner people, perhaps my better angels too.) I confessed how the anxieties of life—and "all of this"—hijacked my desires, how they pulled me toward the bottle. I'd lost my footing for a few solid hours, and here I was, the road to relapse paved with stressor after stressor after stressor.

My friend texted back, asked whether I was still sober. I considered it, wondered how I'd found myself so wrapped up in my nostalgic want of gin that I could only just keep it together. What word was there to describe what I was?

"Soberish," I texted in response.

"Me too," he texted. "Welcome to the human experience."

16. Drink the Wine

One might be tempted to think that by sheer willpower and the application of the Jesus Prayer I managed to overcome temptation, and that by not drinking I'd preserved my sobriety. Sobriety, though, is so much bigger than drinking or not drinking, I think.

I gathered with my tiny church family last Sunday evening. There, we celebrated the death, burial, and resurrection of Christ. The liturgy progressed, pulled me to its apex, where the priest spoke these words: "After supper he took the cup of wine, and when he had given thanks, he gave it to them and said, 'Drink this, all of you: this is my blood of the new covenant, which is shed for you and for many for the forgiveness of sins. Whenever you drink it, do this for the remembrance of me.'"

He lifted the chalice, asked that the Spirit of God would somehow move over the surface of the wine, that he would somehow allow us to drink his very lifeblood. We watched the chalice as he lifted it.

Do this for the remembrance of me, by which he meant drink the wine.

And before we processed to the communion rail, that bar where everybody knows my name (and my penchant for wine), the good priest looked at the bread and wine, looked at us, and proclaimed the truth about those elements.

"These are the gifts of God for the People of God. Take them in remembrance that Christ died for you, and feed on him in your hearts by faith, with thanksgiving."

These are the gifts . . . Take them . . . By which he meant drink the wine.

I processed to that rail with my brothers and sisters, my church family, and I took the bread. I took, too, the clay chalice and I drank no small drink. I drank from the deeps of that chalice, drank until I felt the pinch of the wine in my lungs. In that moment, the wine, the thing that so many would say is my poison, became so much more. Was it a reminder of my days of insobriety? Yes. Was it the object of my redemption too? There can be no doubt.

Each time I participate in the liturgical rhythm, I find that slug of communion wine reminds me of my need for deep healing. Somehow, it transubstantiates, becomes for me the blood of my salvation. This miracle of wine becoming grace—it's a compulsion killer, at least for me.

How did I get to this place where I could drink the wine from the chalice? That's a story I'll save for later in this book. But see how the question of sobriety hangs on more than the question, To drink or not to drink? If it were that simple, wouldn't I have been sober on that day by the pond and unsober at the communion rail? (Some would say so, Lord have mercy.) And if I made abstinence from alcohol the thing, wouldn't each Sunday be a reminder of my addiction instead of a miracle of grace? Wouldn't it walk me to the edge of shame? Wouldn't it lead me into exclusion, isolation, or the like?

17. To Run or Not to Run?

We tend to spoil any good thing, human as we are. We turn the gifts of God into coping mechanisms, just like I did wine, and we do it with any old gift. Consider my friend Rich, a good and right man whom I consider the paragon of health. He's a runner, and a darned good one at that. But one morning over coffee he confessed.

"After a stressful day, after a day when I feel like an imposter or a failure or like I'm measuring up short, I put on my shoes and run till I puke."

"Why?" I said, jerking upright, cocking my head to the side.

"Maybe I'm trying to cope by doing something I'm good at? Maybe I'm trying to run away from my problems? I don't really know."

And therein lies the problem. Running itself isn't the problem. Running away is.

To run or not to run? That is not the question. (I could stand to run a bit more.) But what if the running becomes our way of outpacing our problems, avoiding them, numbing them? Can running become a negative coping mechanism?

WHAT IS THE PROBLEM?

18. THE IMPLICIT RULE OF HUMAN BEING

It's a thing we've all learned, one way or another: it's possible to have an unhealthy relationship with just about anything. It's possible, too, to abstain from those things and still live in the anxiety of a soberish existence. This is the rub of being human in a world of pleasure.

THE BOOK OF WAKING UP

19. To Drink or Not to Drink? That Is Not the Question

If abstinence doesn't necessarily lead to healing and wholeness, and perfectly acceptable (and even good) things can become vices, where does that leave us? I suppose it leaves us in a variation of the classic Shakespearian pickle.

To partake or not to partake? This is not the question.

To prove the point, consider those with socially necessary but disordered habits, addictions, or dependencies. Can they just quit those things?

Can the compulsive shopper quit shopping altogether? If he does, how will he buy food, clothes, and transportation for his family?

Can the compulsive eater stop eating? If she does, how will she survive?

Can the workaholic stop working? If he does, won't he find himself in bankruptcy court?

For so many, abstinence is not a solution. It's not the food or the wine or the shopping or the work that's problematic. The problem lies somewhere deeper, somewhere inside us.

44

20. THE PURPOSE OF STUFF

Why are we prone to turn good things into coping mechanisms? If we don't explore the *why*, we'll substitute one coping mechanism for the other. I know this firsthand. Even in my years of abstinence, stress triggered other compulsions, substitute vices. For me, these substitutes follow my hierarchy of desire:

1. Sex (as much as the confines of holy matrimony will allow)
2. Chocolate, cereal, or cinnamon rolls (the holy trinity of comfort foods)
3. Book buying (fiction, nonfiction, history—*anything* but self-help)
4. The work, work, work (or perhaps it's money, money, money)

You have your own hierarchy of desires, the materials, actions, or habits you tend to use in times of stress. And like alcohol, these materials, actions, and habits (the "Stuff of Earth" as songwriter Rich Mullins once called them) are not evil in and of themselves. The Stuff of Earth has a specific purpose.

21. The Sacramental Nature of the Stuff of Earth

Consider the objects of our desires: sex, chocolate, alcohol, shopping, work, food, even narcotics. Ask yourself, Why *do* you turn to them in times of stress? What do they have in common? You might give any number of answers, but when you boil them down to the bones, you're left with pretty simple soup. Sex, chocolate, alcohol, shopping, work, food, narcotics—they all produce pleasure.

Mmmm, pleasure.

We're coded for pleasure. We have millions of synapses meant to fire, meant to tell the brain to release four neurotransmitters associated with pleasure: dopamine, oxytocin, serotonin, and endorphins. What do those neurotransmitters do? That's not so important for now. Instead, just know this: each plays a part in producing the whizz-bang rush of pleasure we all know. It's this whizz-bang that sets us apart from machines, that makes us human. But why do we feel this pleasure? What's the point of it?

Pleasure—what is it but a sign that our Creator wants us to enjoy the created things of the world?

Pleasure—what is it but a conduit to experience the goodness of God in the land of the living?

Pleasure—what is it but an icon, a portal meant to draw us into the life and love of God? This is the poor-man's working definition of the ten-dollar word *sacramental*.

As Alexander Schmemann puts it in his book *Eucharist: Sacrament of the Kingdom,* God's creation has a certain sacramentality. He writes, "For the world was created and given to man for conversion of creaturely life into participation in divine life." God didn't create pleasure for the fun of it. God created pleasure so our everyday lives would be filled with signs of the divine.

22. THE SACRAMENTAL SPECIFICS

Sex. Isn't there a certain sacramental purpose to it? Doesn't it bring us into participation with the divine life? From the beginning of time, sex has been seen as the consummate act of marriage, the point at which two bodies join in mystical union. What's more, isn't the whizz-bang of sex a prerequisite for our participation with God in the divine act of creation itself, the bringing about of new life?

Work—could it have a sacramental purpose? Sure enough. If we use our vocations as ways of partnering with God to cultivate the world, ways of joining him to provide for our needs and the needs of our families in love, our work is full of sacramental purpose.

Nature? Consider the whizz-bang at the base of your brain when you smell the flowers in spring. Don't they remind you to appreciate the handiwork of a God who created a beautiful world for you? Doesn't the beauty of April conjure primal memories of the first garden, the garden where God woke men and women to love?

Narcotics—there can't be a sacramental purpose to drugs. Right? Wrong. I've watched a man burning with bone cancer slide into the peaceful arms of eternity by way of a morphine drip. The morphine ship that carried him to the far shore of life, didn't it draw him into the arms of God?

Bread and wine—aren't they imbued with a certain kind of sacramentality? Most certainly. Through the pleasures of bread and wine (especially when there's cheese involved), God allows us to taste what's good. Through bread and wine, God invites us to participate in and remember his sacrificial love too (Luke 24:35), a truth I experienced in my own season of waking. What could be more sacramental than bread and wine?

23. A Caveat on Sacramentality

Granted, this is not to say that all things are sacramental in and of themselves. Though sex is imbued with a certain sacramentality, though it can be used in a sacramental way, that sacramentality can also be destroyed by humankind.

How? Consider pornography, virtual sex with a virtual body. Does pornography draw us into God's love, or is it a form of human consumption for self-gratification? Do the secret clicks bring life, or something more akin to the shame of Eden, the shame of being found naked and ashamed? If it's the latter, how can we say it's sacramental?

What about crack cocaine? Is it sacramental? Sure, it relieves pain in a whizz-bang rush, but it destroys the body, sucks the life out of the addict, hastens death. So although crack is made from natural elements created by God, can it be said to have a sacramental nature? I wouldn't go that far.

24. SACRAMENTAL OR NONSACRAMENTAL: WHO DECIDES?

On a gray morning at Puritan Uptown, I shuffle to the bar, drop my bag onto the floor without ceremony. It has been my office over the past few days as I sort through this sacramental conundrum: How does one determine whether anything—sex, food, shopping, whatever—is sacramental?

The barista slides coffee across the bar and I slouch over it, steam warming my nose. Is this coffee sacramental? What about the peanut butter and banana toast I'll order in an hour? The strawberry turnover behind the glass case? The muffin? The water? The Burton's soft-serve ice cream in the machine across the way?

Sacramental or nonsacramental—who decides? I consider the catechetical definition given to my mother in her Episcopal childhood: "A sacrament is an outward and visible sign of an inward and invisible grace." An opaque, esoteric definition if I do say so myself.

Seth Richardson, an Anglican priest, rounds the corner, sits at the bar behind me. He unpacks his things, pulls out his iPad (sacramental or non?), and begins typing. I walk to where he's sitting, hijack the work he's about to do, and toss the conundrum his way.

"How can you tell whether any object, any material, is being used sacramentally?"

He sits, blinking. Working out the question somewhere behind his eyes. We exchange some banter, hazard some guesses, give some examples.

Can porn be sacramental?

What about weed?

Pastries or cereal?

Are there things that fall in a gray area?

Idea tennis—this is what we do, serve and volley questions as we try to come to the point. After a few minutes, a few revisions, he formulates an answer that sticks.

THE BOOK OF WAKING UP

THE BOOK OF WAKING UP

"When we're reaching for a fix, especially one of the big fixes, I think we have to ask, 'Does my attachment to this thing lead to my flourishing *and* the flourishing of others?' If it does, it's full of sacramental grace and purpose. If not?"[1]

There it is, the practical answer to the question. Does the fix lead to deeper communion with God, with your spouse, your children, your community? Does it lead to something more akin to life, or is it a fix that's twisted to death?

---

1   In connection with this conversation, Richardson referenced the work of William Cavanaugh, who offered what can be couched only as criticism of Leonardo Boff's book, *Sacraments of Life, Life of Sacraments.* According to Cavanaugh, Boff's book contains a chapter titled "My Father's Cigarette Butt as Sacrament." In a footnote, Cavanaugh comments, "Boff reports with no apparent irony that the sacramental cigarette in question was the last one (of many) his father smoked before dying of a coronary thrombosis."

25. THE LIFE OF CHRIST SPEAKS OF SACRAMENTALITY

If the life of Christ shows us anything, it's that the Stuff of Earth is meant to point us to the substance of heaven. How? Consider the way he came eating and drinking.

Jesus' best buddy, John, set out to record the life of Christ, miracles and all, and what was the first miracle he recorded? It was a sacramental miracle, one in which Jesus used creation to draw attention to the Creator. Exercise your scriptural imagination with me.[2]

A rabbi, a tax collector, and a fisherman walk into a bar where a wedding party is celebrating the vows of a new marriage. But as the entourage makes its way to the hors d'oeuvres line, the rabbi's mother (a party guest) interrupts, wringing her hands. The wine has run dry, she says. Fix it, Jesus, she says. Jesus (the rabbi) points to the water jugs by the door, the kind used in purification ceremonies. Take the purification jugs, he says, the jugs reserved for holding the cleansing water. Fill them to the brim. Go find the sommelier, he says. (Maybe they spoke French; who's to say?) When the sommelier arrives, the rabbi asks him to draw a drink from the jugs, and when the man does, what does he find? The good stuff, full-bodied. The best wine of the wedding.

See the miracle? Jesus took the water in those jugs, jugs which were kept around to remind the partygoers of their need for purification, and replaced it with good, strong, whizz-bang-inducing drink. The water of the purification was replaced by the pure wine of a new reality. But Jesus didn't create wine for the sake of creating

---

2   I was first acquainted with the term *scriptural imagination* while watching a YouTube video published by the Duke Divinity School. In the video, Dean Richard Hays defines scriptural imagination as "the capacity . . . to see the world through lenses given to us in Scripture." See https://www.youtube.com/watch?v=hTOVoWbRcoA&t=229s.

wine. It was a sacramental transformation meant to point those who witnessed it to the divine care of a loving God.

"Emmanuel," Mary might have said as she witnessed the miracle. "God with Us."

God with Us, who came creating new wine.

God with Us, the source and solution of a party of problems.

God with Us, who came caring about his fellow wedding guests.

God with Us, a man inviting us to a wedding where sacramental wine never runs dry.

26. THE LIFE OF CHRIST SPEAKS OF SACRAMENTALITY AGAIN AND AGAIN

Over and over again, Christ used the whizz-bang-producing Stuff of Earth—water, wine, bread—as means of drawing us deeper into the cosmic communion. Consider the bread he broke, the wine he poured at the Last Supper. They were both the Stuff of Earth, but through them, he drew us into a divine reality. On the night he was betrayed, he took the bread, broke it, and said it was his body. Likewise, he took the wine and said it was his blood (Luke 22:19–20). The disciples didn't have eyes to see in the moment, but Christ was using the materials of earth as sacramental objects, objects meant to pull them into his story, into his divine, sacrificial, all-satisfying love.

Even after his death and resurrection, Christ used the same bread and wine as an invitation into the divine reality. Recall the two followers of Christ who were making their way to Emmaus when a somehow-masked Christ met them. Remember how Christ walked with them, how he shared a village table with them that evening, how he broke the bread and poured the wine. In that shared meal made of earthly stuff, Luke records how Jesus revealed who he was: "Jesus was recognized by them when he broke the bread" (Luke 24:35).

27. I Am the Sacrament

Bread and wine—these are, perhaps, the most poignant examples of how Jesus used the Stuff of Earth to point to the Creator, how he used it as an invitation to draw us into the love of God. But consider, too, Christ's use of language, how he described himself as the objects of creation (that same Stuff of Earth) to help us understand and draw deeper into his love.

I am the light of the world, he said.

I am the bread of life, he said.

I am the vine, the water, the friend, the ultimate truth.

He used the language of created things, the language of pleasure, to point to himself.

28. THE QUESTION WORTH THE PRICE OF A SOUL

Christ used the pleasures of life to point us to the God who loves us, cares for us, satisfies us, and who wants to draw us deeper into participation with him. And it's not hard to imagine God using other pleasures of life—working, buying, selling, making babies, whatever—to point us to the Divine Love, is it? It's not hard to imagine him creating those pleasures at the foundation of the world and crying out, "These are the gifts of God for the people of God. Thanks be to God!"

See? God so loved the world that he gave us the whizz-bang, that whosoever pays attention to the whizz-bang might not miss the point of this one life but might be drawn deeper into the Divine Love. If this is true, then why do we so often adore the pleasures of God as ends instead of as the means of drawing deeper into God's love? Why do we turn these pleasures into coping mechanisms?

29. Screwtape Logic

In *The Screwtape Letters*, C. S. Lewis's fictitious work on devils, humans, and the mud holes of sin we're so prone to waller in, Lewis imagines just how the whizz-bang-inducing scent of a rosebush can be fashioned into something more akin to a crown of thorns. In the narrative, Screwtape, the veteran tempter, writes letters to his nephew and rookie devil, Wormwood. Screwtape offers advice to Wormwood, shares how the devil minor might draw his patient into the southern lake of fire. In one of those letters, Screwtape discusses the sacramental pleasures of God:

> [God's] a hedonist at heart. All those facts and vigils and stakes and crosses are only a facade. Or only like foam on the seashore. Out at sea, out in His sea, there is pleasure, and more pleasure. He makes no secret of it; at His right hand are "pleasures for evermore." Ugh! I don't think He has the least inkling of that high and austere mystery to which we rise in the Miserific Vision. He's vulgar, Wormwood. He has a bourgeois mind. He has filled His world full of pleasures. There are things for humans to do all day long without His minding in the least—sleeping, washing, eating, drinking, making love, playing, praying, working. Everything has to be *twisted* before it's any use to us. We fight under cruel disadvantages. Nothing is naturally on our side.[3]

It's a work of fiction, sure, but doesn't it ring true? The things created by God—the Stuff of Earth—don't always lead to dependency, attachment, or addiction. (I'm not addicted to wine at the moment, for example.) But through Screwtape's subtle twisting of

---

3   C. S. Lewis, *The Screwtape Letters* (New York: Simon and Schuster, 1996), 83.

the pleasures, we come to chase the whizz-bang instead of the giver of the whizz-bang. And when we lose sight of the purpose of the whizz-bang, when we elevate the created over the Creator, the pleasure becomes its own dead end.

30. SCREWTAPE INSIDE ME

It's Screwtape's twisting and hijacking of pleasures that causes us to turn the Stuff of Earth into coping mechanisms. What's more, when I get rid of one coping mechanism, it's the twisting that brings seven other compulsions to take its place (Matt. 12:45).

I've killed my compulsion toward alcohol (even if I still fantasize about it from time to time), but now I'm a workaholic.

When I get on top of my workaholism, I find myself binge-eating Rice Chex at night.

Now that I've righted my relationship with Rice Chex (you devil temptress!), I'm mired in social media or Netflix binges or work or buying stuff I don't need.

Having beaten back all these other coping mechanisms, why do I find myself reaching for everyone's approval?

Why can't I shake the sneaky Stuff of Earth, even when the whizz-bang it produces never satisfies me?

Maybe it's the devil inside me.

Whoa.[4]

---

4   This line—"The Devil inside me, whoa"—is the culmination of The Oh Hellos song "Dear Wormwood," from their 2015 album of the same name. This album, together with their albums *Notos* and *Eurus*, comprised a portion of the soundtrack for the writing of this book. It's also worth mentioning that Typhoon's *White Lighter* and their incredible masterwork *Offerings* were on heavy rotation through the composition of the manuscript.

31. THE CIRCLE OF DESIRE

So many of us think we can beat Screwtape's gambit by using good-old-fashioned, white-knuckled resistance and a soul full of good intentions. We imagine we can quit our coping mechanisms, go off the sauce *du jour* cold turkey. Those good intentions are as thin as the morning spiderwebs, though—sticky but not strong—and they don't stand a chance when compared with the rush of our desires. You know this, don't you? Consider a modern American family, how they prove the point.

Case Study No. 1: A professional shopper (ahem) promises her husband she'd never go into hock over a pair of shoes. See her at the tail end of the workweek, best intentions sagging down around her ankles, credit card with a little limit. In the designated aisle of Macy's, watch her leave her good intentions on the showroom floor.

Charge, charge, charge—it feels so good in the moment. Doesn't it numb the stressors of life?

Case Study No. 2: An attorney was raised in a home with a verbally abusive father. "Toughen up," he was told, "or you'll never be enough." His firm values the billable hours, and this week, he's just a few hours short. On a Friday, he promises his wife (the professional shopper) he'll be home at 5:00, despite being low on hours. He's firm in his commitment, strong in his resolve. Until she calls (from the sales rack at Macy's) to tell him she has a few errands to run. "Don't worry about it," he says, and his anxiety melts as he realizes he's just bought another hit of work.

Case Study No. 3: A teenage boy waits at home for his mother (the professional shopper) and his father (the well-meaning attorney). He's looking forward to dinner, to connection, even if he never knows quite what to say to his preoccupied parents. Always preoccupied. Forever preoccupied with work or new clothes or the "adult conversations" of some new financial scarcity. Bored, he reaches for his phone, pulls up a new screen, types the web address he's sworn off a hundred times. Swipe, swipe, swipe, scanning all the bodies. Picking the right one. Losing himself to the euphoria of satisfied curiosity.

So often, willpower is no match for desire.

32. The Catechism of Humanity

Try as we might to ignore these coping mechanisms, let's call the truth the truth: our desire for the Stuff of Earth is often so much stronger than our will to resist it. Even if each of the subjects in our model American family were able to grit their teeth and claw themselves to the other side of their coping mechanisms, wouldn't they find others hiding in the shadows? Don't so many of us follow the catechism of desire, that sneaky teaching of our DNA?

The Catechism of Desire

Q: What is the purpose of humans?
A: *The purpose of humans is to seek the Stuff of Earth.*

Q: What is the purpose of the Stuff of Earth?
A: *The purpose of the Stuff of Earth is to bring us the whizz-bang.*

Q: What is the whizz-bang?
A: *The whizz-bang is the quick hit of relief, the momentary fix, the feel-good rush.*

Q: What would you leverage to get the whizz-bang?
A: *I would leverage anything to get the whizz-bang.*

Q: What if you feel guilty about the particular kind of whizz-bang you experience, like the whizz-bang of secret sex?
A: *If I feel guilty about the particular whizz-bang I experience, I'll find another kind of whizz-bang.*

Q: What if you try to quit the more destructive habits, the habits that bring a more illicit whizz-bang?

A: *If I try to quit the more destructive habits, I probably won't. Even if I do, I'll find others to replace them.*

Q: Where will you find another compulsive habit to replace your need for the whizz-bang?
A: *Enter Screwtape.*

33. "AVOID THIS QUESTION, PLEASE" (SCREWTAPE)

You know the needling voice of Screwtape, how he twists the pleasures, catechizes us with desire. He whispers deep in the inner ear, *One more time; one more time; come on, just one more time.* These whispers come and come, morph into a sort of vampire song, one that sucks the will from you: *You can sneak this drink, this peek, this pill. One little thrill won't hurt. It'll make you feel good.* These are the songs that lead us to another Jack and Coke, another pill, another one-click deal on Amazon, another smut site, another golden calf we didn't think we'd bow to.

If this isn't you, great. But if you're anything like me or the Israelites or the rich young ruler or the Pharisees or the billions of humans who preceded you, the billions of humans who listened to Screwtape's siren song, consider digging a little deeper. Ask yourself these questions:

- What compulsion sings to me round the clock, begging me to hum along?
- Why can't I shut the song off?
- Is it because the song distracts me from some stressor, some pain, some discomfort?

There it is. The problem. The question that leads to another question: What is the pain?

WHAT IS THE PAIN?

Thorn in my side, pain I can't hide . . .
Feels like I'm headed for a breakdown.

—RYAN ADAMS, "BREAKDOWN"

34. A Man Whose Name Was Paine

In the waning years of his life, I had the privilege of knowing a real holy man named John Paine.[1] There is a disquieting stillness when you sit with a holy man. There—in his office, on his back porch, in his bedroom, wherever—stillness is acute, sharp, maybe a needle point. It's the stillness that pushes through skin, muscle, bone, and marrow into the very center of something. (The heart? The soul?) The holy man knows who he is, and he rests in the way and shape of his life. The student or novice or receiver (in this instance, me) does not know the way or shape of holiness but instead fumbles to hold the weight of any wisdom. Holy men smile at this fumbling. They know that fumbling leads to holding, at least in time. (Just as it is with children, it takes time to develop the capacity for holding.)

"I have amyotrophic lateral sclerosis (ALS) or Lou Gehrig's disease," he said, pausing every two words so that his BiPAP machine could push oxygen into his lungs. "After my diagnosis, they gave me two to five years to live. That was sixteen years ago. I've lost the use of my fingers, toes, arms, and legs. The pain is insufferable. All of it—the pain, the loss of function and mobility—it killed the man I used to be, the one who was in control of everything."

Here sits the dead man walking.

In the days of learning to love Paine, I watched a great well of wisdom suffer suffocation. In that slow slide, I had the great privilege of speaking with him each week, and on one of those calls, he told me of his creeping pain. "My nerves are lit up these days," he said, "and I can't move to soothe them. In the night, I feel like one thousand bugs are crawling across my skin. It's enough to drive you mad." He was considering clipping the nerves, he told me. The

---

1 You can read more of John's story in his book, *The Luckiest Man: How a Seventeen-Year Battle with ALS Led Me to Intimacy with God.*

specialists at Northwest Medical Center could identify the nerve branch giving him trouble, could find the root of that branch in the spinal cord and could cut it clean. It is as easy as cutting a limb from a tree, he said.

"There's only one problem. Without the nerves, I can't feel the pain. Without the pain, I can't tell whether my skin is rubbing raw or whether there's too much pressure on any area of my body. Without the pain, how will I know if a bedsore is working its way to the surface?"

He paused.

"Did you know an infected bedsore can kill you in less than seven days?"

The pain—it was a signaler, and an important one. The pain kept him aware, attuned to his body, to the places he needed treatment. Without the pain, wouldn't he be at risk?

35. The Gift of Pain

This is the way of holy men: they give the facts to you straight, draw you into their stories; then they blindside you with the truth below the facts.

"Physical pain is a curse, but it's sort of a gift too. Isn't it?" John asked.

He paused for effect.

"Is emotional pain any different?" he asked. "Isn't emotional pain a gift too? Isn't it a sign that we need treatment? Isn't it a signaler, an opportunity to invite the great God of healing and comfort to be with us?"

Pause.

Rewind.

"Isn't it a signaler, an opportunity to invite the great God of healing and comfort to be with us? For so long I nursed my emotional wounds in silence. I pushed back the abusive words of my father, the ways he made me feel I'd never measure up. And what did I do to try and deaden those emotional nerves? I worked and worked and worked, as if that might make me enough. What do others do? Shop, eat, drink, whatever. I wish I would have stopped and listened to the signals."

These were his words, not mine, but couldn't I have said something similar about my life, how I'd used alcohol and any number of other things to push back the pain? Though the substances and pains might vary, couldn't we all say something similar?

36. PAIN IS PAIN

I sat in a porch chair on John Ray's deck, fingers tapping against the side of a sweating whiskey glass, head as stable as a top losing its spin. I was sit-down drunk.

It was 2012, and my youngest son, Titus, had been battling an unknown illness, some demon disease. He was an infant, losing weight, failing to thrive. The doctors were at a loss. John knew all this, pastor and friend as he was, and he suffered my search for the bottom of every bottle. He suffered my suffering.

To the best of my recollection (which, I confess, might be blurred by Father Time and Brother Whiskey), I was equal parts sobbing and cussing, a mess of emotions sitting in a deck chair around a fire pit. I was spitfire and vitriol, booze and bile, bored with the sparks jumping at my jeans. These were the days of my existential pain, the pain working itself out in questions, if not outright doubt.

Who was God if not a healer?

Where was God if not present?

Was God, even?

It was spit and vinegar, and in the middle of my whiskey-fueled tirade, I woke to my myopia. Midstream, I stopped my lamentation and considered my friend, John, sitting across the fire pit from me. Hadn't he lost his daughter too soon?

She was a child, only six.

She was exercising her girlish enthusiasm, running through a crosswalk.

There was an intoxicated driver.

There were emergency responders.

There were a hospital visit, tough decisions, a funeral.

Even in my self-indulgent inebriation, I considered his tragedy, the grief of a family, the permanency of death's rot. It was smelling salts, pulling me from my drunken grief.

"I'm sorry," I said, rubbing my eyes and drying my hands on my jeans. "What you went through was . . ."

I couldn't bring myself to tell him how much worse he had it. But John, with the sober wisdom of years on his side, shook his head, said, "There's no reason to apologize. Pain is pain, even when it takes different shapes. And no matter the shape, it still hurts."

37. PAIN THE PYRO

John Ray was right. The problem of pain is that it's pain. It hurts, no matter how much you pretend otherwise. You can try your best to ignore it, to explain it away, or to distract yourself from it, but nerves are real things. Once lit, they're as autonomous as the short fuses of a firecracker. They do what they were created to do. They spit sparks, carry fire to the brain, explode in a rush of chemicals.

Pain is a pyromaniac.

38. EMOTIONAL PAIN: POETRY OR PRECISION?

Emotional pain—"emotional wounds," as Paine called them—those difficult to pinpoint feeling fires are real things. Aren't they? You know it, don't you? It's the deep itch, an ache in the middle of your marrow, the constant buzz of overactive anxiety. It's something real, but difficult to explain. But why do we call it pain?

Dr. Gabor Maté, a clinical physician at the Portland Hotel, a treatment center for those dealing with addiction, shares the connection between physical and emotional pain in his book *In the Realm of Hungry Ghosts*. He writes, "The very same brain centers that interpret and 'feel' physical pain also become activated during the experience of emotional rejection: on brain scans they 'light up' in response to social ostracism just as they would when triggered by physically harmful stimuli. When people speak of feeling 'hurt' or having emotional 'pain,' they are not being abstract or poetic but scientifically quite precise."[2]

Dr. Maté, a bona fide physician, gives us the skinny. The experience we call emotional pain is, in a very real sense, *real*. And the experience of this kind of pain doesn't mean you're broken or weak or needy. It means your brain is doing what it was designed to do—feel. The experience of emotional pain means you're human.

2   Gabor Maté, *In the Realm of Hungry Ghosts: Close Encounters with Addiction* (Berkeley: North Atlantic Books, 2008), 36.

39. THE ANATOMY OF PHYSICAL PAIN

The description of pain as a short-fused firecracker is not all that farfetched, biologically speaking. Consider physical pain. A slap, pinch, or cut is a match to the fuse. Nerve bundles are the fuse. The fuse carries the fire to the brain, where pain receptors explode in a grand chemical reaction.

Studies in Pain No. 1 (the Physical Stuff): It's Spaghetti Tuesday, and you're in the kitchen chopping onions. The sharp knife is in the dishwasher, and so you're using the old blunt-bladed butcher knife. The blade slips from the onion skin, glides down its slick side, and cuts the next best thing it can find—your thumb. Blood comes hard and fast, and after the millisecond of shock dissolves, nerve synapses are lit, and that fire rips a line up the nerves in a millisecond. The sparks gather in the spinal cord, then light an even larger fuse. Faster, faster, faster the pain signal burns up to the brain, exploding in particular areas. It's these brain explosions that signal the need for attention—a bandage, a hospital run, maybe stitches. The pain triggers an emotional response too—the flailing, the crying, the cussing in front of the children. (Oh, come on. It's not just me. Right?)[3]

---

3   For the neurologically curious, among the parts of the brain where pain registers are the anterior insular cortex (the AIC), where the brain measures the size of the explosion, and the anterior cingulate cortex (the ACC), where our emotional response to that explosion is triggered. Though I don't name them in the following sections, these two areas of the brain are triggered during emotional pain too.

40. The Anatomy of Emotional Pain

"This is all fine and good," you say, "but the pain I feel is not that of a cut thumb. It's something deeper, something below the skin."

Emotional pain. The pain of rejection. The pain of loss. The pain of abuse.

This, I suppose, is a fair point. But if physical pain can be characterized as a short-fused firecracker, emotional pain might be commercial-grade dynamite. Consider the words of Dr. Maté again. Those same brain centers that light up when we cut our thumbs? They explode when we experience emotional pain too.

But how is the fuse of emotional pain lit?

41. THE ANATOMY OF EMOTIONAL PAIN

Studies in Pain No. 2 (the Existential Stuff): As a child, your father flew AWOL, packed his car and headed for Lord-Knows-Whereville. He left you and your mother to fend for yourselves, and times were always tight.

Where is Dad? Why'd he leave? Where are the groceries coming from? These were the questions that left their mark on your childhood. And though it's been twenty years since you left your mama's house, the questions still haunt.

You and your husband have a good tussle, a real verbal knock-down-drag-out, and there they are. *Will he leave me too? How will I provide for the children? Does anyone love me? Really?*

There is some sort of button below your skin, and your husband has pushed it without knowing. That button sends an electric current through the same neural pathways used by your body when you cut your thumb last week. The spinal cord carries these signals up and up until chemicals combust in the AIC and the ACC in one God-awful *whoompf.* It's not a cut finger, but it still hurts. That's when the pain responses come—the flailing, the crying, the cussing in front of the children.

The brain, the pain—it's all intertwined.

42. THE PAIN EAST OF EDEN

It'd be nice if Eden were our reality, if we lived in an endless, pain-less spring. It'd be you and me, Adam and Eve, walking in the cool of the evening with God, barefoot, no spurweed stickers hitching rides between our toes. We'd live in the garden west of exile, west of murder, west of pain. Imagine the bliss.

But bliss is not the shape of our story.

Eden was primed with possibility, both the possibility for life and the possibility for pain. Our forerunners explored those possibili-ties, and through the simplest act of disobedience, they introduced pain to the world.

The Snake: Take of this apple and eat. This is the apple of
a new possibility.
Eve, Adam: Thanks be to the snake!

Pain came as they bit into that forbidden fruit. It took the shape of teeth marks, of shame, of fig-leaf coverings, of a shirt made from a slaughtered lamb. Now, all these millennia later, pain takes the shape of the rotten fruit always growing in our own gardens east of Eden. The pain follows us from the beginning to the end.

Through the pain of another we come screaming into the world, faces smooshed flat and heads squeezed through a too-narrow canal. Within minutes of our first breaths, we feel the first pinprick. Our lives are marked by more pinpricks, both physical and emotional, and at the end of it all, pain is the vehicle that leads us to the afterlife.

43. BRAINS ON FIRE

Pain is the potential of human existence. Whether physical or emotional, this potential explodes again and again throughout the course of our lives. Broken bone? Explosion. The death of your childhood dog? Explosion. Divorce? Explosion. A rejection letter from your college fallback option? Explosion. Verbal abuse? Explosion. Lost job, death of a child, a fight with your friend, a rumor circulating about you at the church or office, a cancer diagnosis? Explosion, explosion, explosion, explosion, explosion.

If life is good at anything, it's setting the brain on fire, and though it might be easy to douse those fires for a time with the Stuff of Earth, we might consider a different approach. We might see these brain fires as signal fires, as leading us to the place of our needs, the different shapes of our pain, as John Ray said.

44. SHAPE OF PAIN 1: SCARCITY

In my childhood, I was carried to a faith healer. Maybe he didn't know he was hawking snake oil, but he hawked it nonetheless, promising if I had enough faith, God would deliver me from asthma, maybe unravel and recode my DNA. I prayed along with him, carried faith as only a child could. But then? The healing didn't come. And what took the place of that healing?

The existential pain of unanswered faith.

I read between the lines, the way all children do.

My faith was not enough.

My experience of God was not enough.

I was not enough.

Those were the days when the doubt set in, and I carried my fractured faith through my childhood years, and then my scarce one through my teen years. By my twenties, I'd learned to fake a steady, sure faith. (Play along; play along; who will know the difference?) Then, in my thirties, when my youngest son fell ill, everything shook, steady though I might have appeared to be. I struggled to speak with a God I'd never found to be a comfort, a healer, present. That's when the familiar childhood ache set in.

I was not enough. I'd never been enough. My not-enoughness might cost my son his life.

There it was, the shape of my pain: scarcity. Scarcity had taken the shape of unanswered prayers.

45. SHAPE OF PAIN 2: ABUSE

In the fall of 2016, I shared my story of pain—the pain of scarcity—with a group of MOPS moms in Milwaukee. I shared how that scarcity scooped a hole in my guts, how it hollowed me out, and how a proper hollowing out is a painful thing. It led me to my numbing mechanisms, I told them, the way I boozed myself to sleep so I didn't have to feel my pain.

I said the last amen and made my way to the side of the stage, where a woman was already waiting. Her eyes were veiny; even in the dim lighting I could tell as much. Her face was puffy. The loose ends of a handful of tissues poked from her balled-up fist, and the frayed tips trembled. She moved in close enough for me to smell her lilac perfume, the Vicks on the tissue, the whiff of last night's bottle.

"Percocet and whiskey," she whispered on the third try.

I knew.

"What is the pain?" I asked.

"My stepfather. In the midnight hours, he visited me, he took advantage of me, he shushed me, shut me up, isolated me. It's been twenty years, so why do I still carry so much guilt and shame? Why was I ever guilty in the first place? I know it wasn't my fault, but still, I feel like I'm walking around with a spike in me."

"I'm sorry," I said, because what else is there to say to a woman who's suffered the worst depravity man can muster? I stood there with her in the pain, held her confession for a minute. I wondered aloud, had she visited a therapist or counselor? No, she said, because talking about the abuse meant seeing her stepfather's face again and again and again. To see his face meant to feel his wandering hands, to smell his breath. To feel his hands, to smell his breath meant to feel the spike. To feel the spike brought thoughts of self-harm, of suicide. Pills—those seemed to dull the memories, the thoughts of dying.

Abuse takes the shape of a stab wound. Maybe a hundred stab wounds. Perhaps a thousand.

46. Shape of Pain 3: Loss

"In the fall, I'm prone to fits of depression and booze."

He's never said these words to me, not in such a direct way. I can still read between the lines, though.

Wes was too young when death hollowed out his dad's bones, so young that the man was more like a superhero or demigod to Wes than a father. Wes adored him, maybe even worshiped him. Every year, in the same season, Wes remembers the casket, the wake, the lowering of the body into the ground. Now, almost thirty years later, he nurtures the memory of that loss when the leaves go gold. There is the acute sense that he is alone, even here in the Ozarks, God's country.

The pain of loss. It takes the shape of the space the cancer hollowed out.

47. HOW SHAPES OVERLAP

Scarcity, abuse, and loss—these are the shapes of so much of our pain. I might propose that emotional, existential pain takes one of these shapes, and that some events create the shape of more than one kind of pain.

Shape Begets Shape Begets Shape (a Practical Example): The father had a good job, a money manager in the financial services industry. He was competent, disciplined, the last person you'd expect to have a hidden drinking problem. Then the financial crisis hit in 2008, the pressure of client expectations, the thinning income. The five o'clock drink became the four o'clock drink, which became the three o'clock drink, and so on. There was a DWI charge over a workday lunch hour. A next-day meeting with the personnel committee. A terminal decision. He drove home wondering how it'd come to this, the loss of his dream job. And how was it that he felt so alienated, so alone?

He walked in the back door, told his wife the whole truth. She stood in disbelief. Why did it feel like a fist to the stomach? Perhaps it was a reminder of her alcoholic father, who'd tongue-lashed her for years. Her husband's alcohol abuse dragged up demons of past abuse, and now what was there to do? Would she have to go back to work to knit together some kind of safety net?

Their daughter heard her mother's question—Will I have to go back to work?—from her hiding spot in the other room. The money? Where would the money come from? What about clothes, her cell phone, her allowance?

See? Pain begets pain begets pain. Shape begets shape begets shape. Loss, abuse, scarcity—who knows how many pain shapes are made by a single event?

48. THE NARRATIVES OF PAIN

Pain has a shape, yes. It has a voice too. It spins archetypal narratives.

Scarcity whispers, "There's never enough."

Abuse pounds, "No one is safe."

Loss reminds us, "You're always alone."

These are the narratives of pain, and they haunt, haunt, haunt, especially in the darker hours. And in my darker hours, the hours of my son's sickness, scarcity sneaked into my room, whispered, "Do you think your faith is enough to save your son, to save you? Will you ever have enough faith? Really?" Tired as I was of that voice in that season, I drank myself to sleep, past the point of waking.

Even in these days of sobriety, scarcity still visits me in the midnight hours. These days, though, I don't turn to coping mechanisms to dull my inner ear to her voice. Instead, I've learned to listen, to let her voice point me to the place where I most need healing.

49. WHY SO MUCH WORK ON THE SHAPES OF PAIN?

Why have I spent so much time discussing emotional pain, categorizing it, and examining the message each kind of pain sends? Because over the last few years, I've spent a good deal of time with those mired in their coping mechanisms. On more than one occasion, they've outed the Stuff of Earth they use to silence some kind of anxiety, dull some kind of pain. But on more than one occasion when I've asked what was behind that anxiety, that pain, they couldn't put their fingers on it. They hadn't learned to listen to the narratives, to have those narratives lead them back to the place they needed healing.

50. Do You Know Your Pain?

Maybe you're like so many others who feel the burn but haven't identified the origin of the house fire. Let's do a little forensic work. Let's see what we can uncover.

Take a moment to reflect and ask, "What is the shape of my pain?" And if you can't identify it, try to back your way into it. Ask, "Which of the three archetypal narratives most resonate with me?" When you identify that narrative, dig deeper, ask yourself when you first heard that narrative playing like a broken record in your noggin.

When did the message first take root?

Where were you?

Who was there (other than Screwtape)?

What was the situation?

Grab a journal and make some notes. Consider them. Pray to see the connections. Can you identify the shape of your pain? Have you found the source of it? Can you give it a name?

51. ANOTHER VEHICLE TO GET TO THE PAIN

Maybe you'd say, "I'm sure I have some sort of pain, some sort of underlying wound, but I still can't put my finger on it. I still can't find the locus of the wound."

Fair enough.

Consider this, then. What triggers your anger, fear, resentment, doubt, sorrow, or despair? What memory provokes cussing, tears, or withdrawal? Can you point to your broken feelings?

Stop reading, just for a moment. Try.

These emotions are your subway tunnel. They'll lead you to the place of the pain if you'll let them.

52. Steve and the Emotional Path to Pain

Sitting among friends, Steve—a minister—confessed that his day had spun out of control and that the loss of control was spinning him into a bout of uncontrollable anger.

"I can't quite identify any pain point," he said, "but my anger and blame mechanisms don't feel so healthy. I know there has to be pain underlying this somehow."

It was supposed to be a day full of work, of moving from one appointment to the next, he said. But then his wife called from the park, told him the car engine wouldn't turn over. She was stranded and needed help. Why did this simple request for help from the one he loved the most conjure such resentment?

He jumped into his car, dialed the numbers of his morning appointments. Cancel, cancel, cancel—he canceled all his appointments (including our lunch appointment), and with each cancellation, he felt the weight of guilt setting in. This guilt was his wife's fault somehow. Except it wasn't. He knew better, and yet his wife was such an easy scapegoat.

Another in the group asked when Steve first felt guilt, the first time he turned his guilt to blame shifting.

"I suppose it was in college, when my roommate disrupted my study schedule with . . ." he paused, "whatever. He was the most disruptive human I'd ever met to that point, and each time he threw my schedule out of whack, I blamed him."

"Why was it so important to keep your schedule?" I asked.

"I think it goes back to my childhood. I could never seem to be anywhere on time. On Sundays, even when I was five or six, my mom and dad would walk out the door for Sunday church and sit there, honking, until I climbed into the back seat. We'd ride to church in complete silence, them seething. It's still this way when I go home. I carry so much shame and guilt at always being the late one."

"They blame you, even now?"

"Yeah. These are the moments I feel most alone."

One of the friends, a therapist, broke in. "Is it any wonder, then, that when you're late, when you let someone down, when your schedule is thrown off kilter, you transfer those same emotions onto others? Onto your wife? It's learned behavior to insulate you from feeling your guilt and blame."

"Somehow, I've never really considered that."

His emotional response—the guilt, the shame—led him to the archetypal narrative "I feel alone." The archetypal narrative led him to the shape of his pain—loss.

Emotions—can't they lead us to the discovery of our pain, even the sneakiest, oft-thought innocuous pain?

53. Considering Steve's Story

Steve's example begs a pause. Go ahead. Ask the question you're nursing.

Do you believe minor childhood wounds carry the same emotional gravity as the loss of a child or abuse by a parent or the scarcity of poverty?

Let me be clear: no.

It's true—certain emotional pain is more significant and requires more attention, just like a broken femur requires more attention than a scraped knee. The loss of a parent as a child—who can forget such a thing? Sexual abuse by a predator—how do these wounds ever heal? Finding yourself forever on the business end of structural racism—I can't imagine it. But the point remains—even what seems like insignificant pain can push us to coping mechanisms (like blame shifting).

See the woman carrying the guilt and shame of her abuse into any given day? See her spinning down into depression?

See Jimmy, who lost his brother? See the shape of his loss, the narrative of his aloneness?

See Steve, who suffered a comparatively minor (though recurring) pain? See how that pain continues to haunt him, to plague his relationship with his wife, even today?

When unattended to, pain does what it does—it hurts and hurts and hurts. And human as we are, we'll always look for pain relief. The question, of course, is, Where will we find that relief?

54. NATURE, MEN, AND THE DIVINE REMEDY

Pain is not a discriminator of persons. It does not pick and choose by race, age, gender, or sexual preference. It doesn't discriminate among any organic thing, even nature. Need proof?

Our big brother Paul wrote a letter to the Romans, pagan gentiles who were newcomers to Christianity. He spoke the language of nature, told them that all creation (every organic thing from the spider you just smashed against your bedroom wall, to the landfill where yesterday's spent jeans are buried) groans in pain. He writes, "We know that the whole creation has been groaning in labor pains until now; and not only the creation, but we ourselves, who have the first fruits of the Spirit, groan inwardly while we wait for adoption, the redemption of our bodies. For in hope we were saved" (Rom. 8:22–24 NRSV).

Nature and men, we both groan for pain relief. We both want the same things. What? Adoption into the Divine Love. Redemption of the bodies through the Divine Love. The hope that's rooted in Divine Love. The hope that all created things—even the bread, the wine, the work, the money, whatever—can be pulled into the very nature of God.

55. C. S. Lewis Sums It Up Better Than I Ever Could, but I'll Still Try

We all have pain (every man, animal, vegetable, and mineral), even though those pains may seem different. Recognizing pain can be difficult, admitting pain can be difficult. But there's a purpose behind the pain. C. S. Lewis puts it this way: "We can ignore even pleasure. But pain insists upon being attended to. God whispers to us in our pleasures, speaks in our conscience, but shouts in our pains: it is his megaphone to rouse a deaf world."[4]

Pain is the divine proclamation, the thunderous wakeup call. It shouts to us, "Something is broken!" And if we wake to the call, pain directs us to a proper hope, the hope Paul writes about in his letter to the Romans—incorporation into the Divine Love.

So many of us don't recognize pain's invitation, though. In pain, we don't hear the call of the Creator to enter into Divine Love and find the redemption (or healing) of that pain. Instead, with vision clouded by the smoke of our emotional house fires, we turn to our coping mechanisms, to the Stuff of Earth, hoping the whizz-bang chemicals it produces can buy us a minute of relief. We bow at the altar of the Stuff of Earth. We revel in the Stuff of Earth. And we can't get enough of the Stuff of Earth. We chase it, even if it leads us east of Eden.

What do we call the chase?

---

4   C. S. Lewis, *The Problem of Pain* (1940; San Francisco: HarperSanFrancisco, 2001), 91.

56. Chasing Addictions

Some call our compulsion to chase the Stuff of Earth "addiction," especially when those numbing agents are chemically based. But before you opt out of self-examination saying, "Sure, I might shop a little too much, but shopping isn't an addiction," pause. Isn't it possible to chase things other than booze to kill the pain? Haven't we all turned to all manner of coping mechanisms when the pain came calling? (I'm too tired to pray, but Netflix? Yup.) But is this turning toward coping mechanisms addiction?

WHAT IS ADDICTION, REALLY?

I fled the country
I thought I'd leave this behind.

—TYPHOON, "DREAMS OF CANNIBALISM"

57. What Are Addictions?

The sneaky little habits we engage in over and over, the distractions we tend to minimize, are those really addictions? What are addictions, really?

I could offer scientific or psychological explanations of addiction, show how they are nothing more than our brains' habituated ways of dealing with stress or pain. I could show how addictions are little more than spiritual attachments, ways we seek the anesthetic effects of pleasure instead of turning to the Divine Love, the love that wants to bring healing. I'll do both, of course, but before we turn to science or spirits, let's turn to story.

58. HOOK ME UP, BUTTERCUP

We all know the old saying, "Two things are certain in life—death and taxes." Our fathers, mothers, accountants, preachers, and drinking buddies have all said it. And though I don't like adages as a general rule, this one rings true, though I might simplify it.

One thing is certain in life: pain. (What is tax day but a day of pain? What is death but the culmination of pain?)

And I suppose if there's another thing that's certain, it's that humans will try their darnedest to avoid, numb, or kill the pains of life. Doesn't everyone *need* a drink on tax day? Don't we run opiate IVs into our arms on our dying day? (For the record, when I near the end of my days, hook me up, buttercup.)

59. ADDICTION OR MEDICATION?
PAINKILLERS AREN'T ALL BAD

A Cautionary Word: Don't hear what I'm not saying. I'm not saying that pain numbing is bad or sinful or devil horned *per se*. If we revisit the idea that God has created things with a sacramental purpose, then didn't he give us the ingenuity and elements to create painkillers which sometimes function as a sign of his grace and love? Don't those painkillers sometimes lead to our flourishing? That said, when the created things, the whizz-bang pleasures of any object become our sole solution for pain, the sacramental purpose gets twisted and things get wonky. As in sometimes sideways-walking wonky. That's my story, anyway. (Thanks a lot, Screwtape.)

60. A New Old Story

I told the story as best I could in *Coming Clean: A Story of Faith,* the story of how I nursed the bottle in the hope it would drown out the voice of scarcity. But time changes perceptions, memories, the ways we bend phrases around stories. It brings new epiphanies, new ways of understanding, too. I see my days of overdrinking and my journey to sobriety differently now than I did in 2013. Now I see it as the journey to waking.

61. The Roadmap to a Problem

If the destination is a drinking problem, here was my roadmap for getting there: years of normalish (though sometimes heavy) drinking; then the mounting stress of a job; then the unexpected, dire illness of a son; then a lengthy stint in a children's hospital; then the following months of confusion, of the fear of everything falling off the rails, of anxiety. And in that season of confusion, fear, and anxiety, I turned to the painkiller I'd become well acquainted with through my years of normalish drinking—booze. I drank to silence the pain, the anxiety, the doubt. I drank myself to sleep one night, then one week, then a handful of months, and just like that, I was a functional dependent.

62. The Epiphany of Sobriety

My epiphany was a grace-filled one, one which did not involve a DWI or a bar fight with a barrel-chested redneck or some drunk-and-regret-filled fling with a coworker. Instead, it came quietly in the lobby of a Methodist church in Austin, Texas.

I'd been speaking at a conference, and I'd tied one on the night before, drunk tequila well into the three-o'clock hour. I'd tied one on the night before that too, though my medicine had been whiskey. And the night before? Same story, different booze—gin, vodka, and the dregs of a growler, to be exact—and working that multiple-day hangover (a lavish Christian hangover, to be exact), I stood in the lobby sipping coffee, trying my best to follow a conversation with Daniel, a humanitarian photographer. I wasn't succeeding.

Over the photographer's shoulder, the oversized wooden doors leading into the church opened. Morning sunlight streamed in through those doors, shattered across the stone floor, its shards splitting my head. Against those shards, a silhouette. The doors closed and the silhouette gave way to a face. There she was, my friend Heather King, who'd quit the bottle years ago. She was an icon of possibility.

When faced with icons—people or objects that point us northward—we have options:

Option 1: Avoid the icon, turn tail and run.
Option 2: Burn the icon down, pull it from its pedestal.
Option 3: Allow the icon to direct our attention to something transcendent, some kind of epiphany.

In that moment, option 3 chose me, dragged me across the lobby and led me to Heather. She smiled, said, "Hey!" but I didn't reciprocate.

"How did you know you had a drinking problem?"

The question hung as she searched for some response, as I looked for a way to drag the words back. There was no pretending.

A few awkward seconds ticked by as her sky-blue eyes turned kind. "You know, don't you?" she responded. Maybe I nodded. Maybe I cried. Truth is, I don't recall my response. I recall only this: something like an eye-opening started.

63. MY ANANIAS

I was still sleep-drunk, still blind. Heather was a guide. She shared her story, explained the signs of her own problem drinking: drinking early (check), drinking often (check), drinking a lot (check). She hadn't hit anyone or gotten a DWI or lost a job, she said. She touched my eyes with the experience of her life, and as she did, the scales fell. I could see it: booze—it'd become my drug of choice, my inefficacious medicine, the painkiller that kept me blind to real healing. In the moment of waking, of seeing, I knew the truth.

I had a drinking problem and all of that.

Lord have mercy and all of that.

The morning conversation dragged into noon, into the early evening. And sure as I was, I called Amber and outed myself. I told her the whole truth, how I'd been drinking too much for nights on end. I hadn't told her about the months (years) I'd been meeting coworkers and clients for happy hour drinks on the sly. I hadn't told her I'd been pouring doubles or triples in my gin and tonics. I hadn't told her that when she left the room to go the restroom during any episode of *Fringe,* I made my way to the kitchen, topped off my drink, hoped it'd pull me into some alternate universe where my son's sickness didn't haunt so hard.

Amber listened, asked whether I might be an alcoholic. I wasn't sure the word fit, not yet, anyway. Problem drinker? That was easier language. She held my confession as gently as a child with a glass bluebird. It'd be okay, she said, and she promised she'd toss the booze out before I got home. She didn't once flog me with the Scriptures, didn't heap coals of judgment on me. Instead, she incarnated the words of her Christ: "In this world, you'll have trouble, even dependency, but don't worry, I'll beat it back with you" (John 16:33, my paraphrase).

64. THE SILENCE OF GOD

My confession didn't catch Amber off guard. Not really. All the normal warning signs were there even if she didn't know the whole truth (nothing but the truth, so help her), and in the months before, she'd asked me if I had a problem. She asked if *maybe* I shouldn't quit drinking.

"What if God has something for you? What if you're trying to ruin it?" she asked.

I wasn't sure about God, wasn't sure whether he had anything but silence for me, and when I considered the silence of God, everything burned. It wasn't a metaphorical burning either, not the fire of artistic sentiment. It was a very real, nerve-scorching, nuclear fire, and I knew only one way to make it stop: douse it with booze.

But when I was off the sauce, the fire was unrelenting, and it was that fire that drove me to the therapist's couch for ninety days. And over those ninety days, the therapist led me to an examination of my coping mechanism.

"Why the dependency?" he asked. "What pain are you trying to kill?"

What pain? Sweet Jesus, what pain am I not trying to kill?

How about the pain of my son's potential death?

How about the pain of death that haunts us all?

How about the pain of the silence of God in it all?

65. The Pain beneath the Pain: Recognizing Scarcity

Over those ninety days, I learned to live awake to the pain without turning to the bottle. As I did, I began to see the pain beneath the pain. Sure, the God of the universe wasn't stepping in to heal my son, and this might have been enough, but it wasn't the whole story. The truth is, God hadn't healed me when I most needed it.

With the help of that therapist, I explored my earliest wounding—the childhood asthma, the faith healer, the prayer that healed nothing. The therapist asked the right questions, listened, and helped me identify the thread of existential pain that ran through the center of my life—scarcity. He helped me see how, when scarcity came knocking thirty years later as I watched my son struggle to live, scarcity took up residence in my brain, and this time, she pulled out the razorblades and slashed my brain.[1] When those slashes scrambled my scruples, when the pain became too much, I crawled into a bottle of Gordon's gin.

Gin—the old family friend, the nectar of nostalgia which reminded me of my grandfather, my people, the banks of the family homeplace on a Louisiana bayou—had turned sour.

---

1 This turn of phrase, "slashed my brain," is an homage to William Stafford's poem "Scars." This poem is a worthy companion for any who've struggled with pain, which is to say all of us.

66. The Ninety-Day Experiment

Ninety days. That's what I gave God. In the evenings, I sat in my living room chair with a journal, and I invited the silent God into my pain. I contemplated the pain, asked him to connect with me in it somehow. As mystical or impossible or insane as it might sound, the more I invited him into that pain, the less the animal voice in it howled. The fires burned less hot. Something like peace settled over me. And though I never heard his voice, he was somehow present. In that presentness, a different flame was kindled, the flame of Divine Love.

He didn't fix everything overnight, of course, didn't cure Titus's illness overnight or drop gold from heaven to pay all the hospital bills. He didn't even see fit to give me all the perfect verses at all the perfect times. Instead, he taught me how to be still, even in the darkness. He taught me how to be loved. It wasn't a miracle, but it was close enough.

67. ASLEEP TO THE PROBLEM

In the five years that followed, the Good God showed me how I'd used created things (specifically fermented grains) to numb myself, but liquor wasn't really the problem. The Good God opened my eyes to the Scriptures, the saints, and a slew of good modern psychologists and therapists. Through them, he showed me how I could wake from my drunken stupor into the Divine Love.

68. THE ETYMOLOGY OF ADDICTION

When I describe this season of my life, some are tempted to bypass the nuance and slap labels on me—alcoholic, addict, whatever. I resist these terms because they're layered with implied meaning and laden with baggage. I suppose the terms are instructive. It's true I drank a great deal, enough to pass (fail?) the AA quiz for a potential alcohol problem.[2] I suppose in the classic sense of the word I was addicted. What is the classic sense of the word? If you're an etymology geek like me, buckle up. This is fascinating.

---

2   For the quiz, visit https://www.aa.org/pages/en_US/is-aa-for-you-twelve-questions-only -you-can-answer.

69. What's in a Word?

Addiction. It's a word which originated in connection with the Roman system of slavery bonds. The indebted servant, it was said, was addicted to the service of his creditor.[3] There was a bonded attachment between the two, a tethering of one to the other, a compulsion for the weak to serve the strong. The addict served his master till debt satisfaction did they part. (And though I don't know Roman slave history, if the history of men is any indicator, the addict rarely satisfied his debt to his master.)

In time, the term *addiction* was broadened and made famous by the likes of old Bill Shakespeare, who likened a person's compulsive behavior to being an addict, a slave. And doesn't that make sense? Don't we all feel powerless when we try to kick a rooted habit? When Master Desire comes calling, don't we so often hop to it and obey his commands, even when we don't want to? I know I do.

---

3   I first discovered the definition of *addict* while reading a book about cocaine and Freud I picked up for less than five bucks at the Dickson Street Bookshop, the best used bookshop in America. Come visit me and we'll search for a second copy of the following title together: Howard Markel, *An Anatomy of Addiction: Sigmund Freud, William Halsted, and the Miracle Drug, Cocaine* (New York: Vintage, 2011).

70. We're All Only Human

It's not just me. It's not just you. It's not just the lay people who struggle with addiction. More than a few holy men, holy women, preachers, priests, friars, nuns, and reverent church ladies (even those who kneel before crucifixes or by their bedsides for hours in prayer) are prone to slavery to their desires. Yes, some struggle against it, use the call of desire to press deeper into the Divine Love. Some, though, can't break their bonds. They are, after all, only human.[4]

4 I consider, for instance, Brennan Manning, who I'm not sure ever beat the bottle. Stumbling as he was, though, he taught us all something about the love of God. For that, I'm grateful. *A word to St. Brennan:* There's no judgment here. I hope we can gather round the table and revel in the Divine Love one day.

71. USING *ADDICTION* AS AN INSULATING TERM

If we're honest, so many of us are slaves to our habits, which is by definition *addiction*. But isn't it tempting to use the words *addiction* and *addict* as insulating terms?

The word *addiction* draws a line. The druggies, alcoholics, maybe even sexaholics or compulsive gamblers are addicts in a proper sense. Not us. We're the clean ones, the ones who don't do anything *that* bad. Sure, we might overeat from time to time (which is to say every day), we might engage in a little self-gratification every now and again (which is to say every week), we might overshop some days (which is to say on the first weekend of every month). But we aren't addicts. Right? Addicts take different forms, we believe, some of which follow:

> *Form 1:* the town drunk with the chest-length gray beard hanging over the mustard-stained white tee
> *Form 2:* the heroin-thin lead singer in the local college neopunk band who thinks she's the next coming of Patti Smith, standing on the stage and singing "Jesus died for somebody's sins, but not mine"
> *Form 3:* the hard-charging business man who burns so hot in his coke-fueled, eighteen-hour workday
> *Form 4:* the PTA parent who floats into anything twenty minutes late on a cloud of Percocet
> *Form 5:* the staggering grandfather who reeks of gin

Those people—*they* are the addicts. And the more extreme a picture we paint, the more distance we put between us and them.

Insulating terms and caricatures are handy things. They keep us from confronting the truth of our subtle coping mechanisms. Our slavish bonds. They keep us from confronting God, addicts as we all might be.

72. Avoiding the Language of Addiction

To be clear, I've participated in this same sort of line drawing (some might say name-calling). In the years since I woke from my drunken drowsiness, I've done my best to draw distinctions between my penchant for gin and the fall-down drunkenness of the *real* alcoholics. Remember how I resisted the term *alcoholic* when Amber asked? See how I resist it still? *Dependent* or *dependency* always sounded so much softer or approachable, or at least less permanent. Dependents can still have meaningful, productive lives. Alcoholics lose careers, friends, and family members. Dependents spend time with their therapists. Alcoholics spend time in the clink for drunk driving. Dependents can still be functional. Alcoholics are not.[5]

---

5 These are, of course, false dichotomies. Still, dichotomies make us feel special. Just ask any Auburn football fan living in Alabama.

73. ABUSING THE LANGUAGE OF ADDICTION

We use the term *addiction* to draw lines, but there's a sneakier way to use it, one often employed by gurus, spiritual leaders, and the more self-actualized among us. Consider this example, inspired by actual events.

Example: The Overidentifying Guru: In church, a preacher takes the stage. He is put together, his jeans well pressed, sporting cool kicks. His hair is mussed just enough to give the appearance of commonness, though held in place with what his wife calls product. He is the brand of hip Christian clean that's most coveted among the megachurches in America's geographic south. Best as I can recall (best as anyone can, for that matter), he has never had a dark day of struggle in his life. At least, not a public one.

He stalks the stage in a silent, almost contemplative moment. He moves to center stage, looks straight at the crowd, hands in his pockets. His first words are almost whispered.

"I have a confession."

A confession? From his platform?

"I'm an addict, and I can't help myself. I've tried to stop, but I can't control it. I find myself creating spaces for my addiction, and I've hidden it from so many. From you. It's hard to admit."

Dramatic pause. I consider the options: porn, pills, booze, poker. I brace. The congregation braces. He pulls his hands from his pockets, runs his fingers through his hair, and takes a deep breath. The moment is so taut, if you could pluck it like a string, it'd vibrate in the key of D minor. But the moment isn't plucked. Instead, the theme music for a well-known sports documentary series cuts the tension, and the preacher looks out at the audience, face painted with an aw-shucks grin. Shrugging his shoulders, he pooches his lower lip out like a preschooler asking for another cookie or another hug or another laugh.

"I'm addicted to ESPN's *30 for 30* documentary series."

The congregation chuckles.

Addiction. How cute.

The preacher's confession is an object lesson of some sort, but I can't get past the superfluity of it all. His facade of togetherness is well intact, no matter how he tries to convince me that he's . . . what? Like me?

He must have made some quip, some gesticulation, but I don't hear it over the pounding of my pulse. The people laugh again, at least, most of them. The rest of us—those who've experienced the powerlessness of what he might call an actual addiction—scan the carpet, the walls, the ceiling. We flip through our Bibles or doodle on the giving envelopes. We avoid eye contact with the preacher, the congregant laughing to our left, our spouses, who know our histories.

The addicts in the room realize: our pain is their punchline.

"See," the preacher spins, "we're all the same. All addicts." I don't believe him, though. He doesn't believe himself. He believes that, somehow, he's different. Somehow, I'm different. In a candid moment, he'd admit it: there really *is* a difference between the fella who can't stop clicking through bouncing bodies on the internet and the preacher who throws away an hour a week on sports documentaries. But somehow, in this moment of walled-up, hyperbolic, false vulnerability, I'm supposed to believe that he believes what he's saying.

I don't.

Addiction—he uses the term as a mechanism for overidentifying with the people, but it rings like a ruse. Isn't he implying there really are two kinds of addictions? The harmless ones that draw a laugh—like a good *30 for 30* binge on Netflix—and the sort that land you in the clink? But the devil is in the details of this sort of campy mockery of lesser addictions. It's the sort of mockery that allows a wide swath of well-meaning folks to opt out of self-examination while ostracizing others.

74. A BRIEF PAUSE TO REFLECT

And this, I suppose, is an opportunity to pause to reflect on the notion and nature of addiction.

How do you use the terms *addict* and *addiction?* Do you use them as insulating terms, a way to draw us-versus-them distinctions? Do you use the language of addiction to win a cheap laugh? Do you use the terms of addiction to set yourself apart as someone who's pretty clean, someone who's mastered most of their appetites, except for a few tiny ones that certainly don't qualify as actual-factual addictions, even if you use those appetites without considering the God who gave them to you?

75. WE ARE THE ADDICTS

What if we disabused ourselves of the notion that we're not addicts? What if we stopped long enough to ask whether we overuse the Stuff of Earth, whether we have slavish attachments to some coping mechanism. And what if we understood the neuroscientific realities of how these coping mechanisms form? What if we realized that our compulsive video gaming isn't that much different from the crack addict's compulsion to set fire to tiny rocks? Wouldn't that level the playing field, maybe even fill us with empathy for those we're quick to castigate? Wouldn't that level up our compassion?

We've all answered the call of pleasure in our lives, often in an attempt to silence some want, some desire, some pain. And before you show me your lily-white gloves, know this: science, the Scriptures, literature, and the human experience show we all have dirty hands. We've all ridden our desires to the sweaty end.

76. WHAT IS ADDICTION? CONSIDER THE COPING MECHANISMS

A Human Truth: Desires create tension, want, and they always beg for satisfaction. Our brains use tried-and-true coping mechanisms to satiate those wants and desires. What kinds of coping mechanisms?

Habits. Don't we all have bad habits we can't seem to break? What about the way we stream some podcast, some YouTube video, some new Netflix series (maybe even popular sports documentaries) whenever cold silence sets in?

Affections. In loneliness, haven't we all turned to some affection, something other than God, to mute the pain of that solitude? In moments when we have not loved God with our whole hearts, haven't we loved money, work, or craft beer?

Attachments. You know the feeling of attachment, of fixation on the next idea, the next purchase, the next follower on social media. Consider your cell phone, for instance. When it's attached to your hand, when you're fixed on the screen, doesn't it drag you away from being present to the moment? Doesn't it draw your attention away from your friends, your family, your aspirations and hopes? (Confession: I often open my own virtual escape hatch to a world of social-media avatars during Thanksgiving family visits, a confession of which I'm not proud.)

Dependence. Booze, pills, sugar—those are the objects of dependence, sure. But in seasons, haven't you been dependent on the win-loss record of your favorite sports team or the size of your waist or the sense that the third new pair of cute strapless sandals might somehow satisfy you? Maybe you're dependent on another romp to brighten your outlook? Maybe another pull of the slot-machine lever or another credit-card swipe at the Target checkout will satisfy your financial woes? Maybe you're dependent on the right theology to give you status in a certain community? And if you're not quite sure how to measure dependence, ask yourself this: Am I able to shake the temptation to use whatever it is, or do I always give in?

See how so many of our coping mechanisms sound a great deal like addiction? See how we all might be addicted to something?

WHAT IS ADDICTION, REALLY?

77. I'M POWERLESS TOO

Often, habits, affections, attachments, and dependencies lead you around by the nose, just as cocaine leads the hardcore drug user. If you were honest with yourself in a moment of quiet consideration, you'd admit just how powerless you are to stop these things you'd rather not do, especially when the pain narratives come knocking.[6] Right? There's a scientific reason for this. It's what developmental psychologist Dr. Marc Lewis calls the biology of desire.

---

6   "There's never enough," "No one is safe," "You're always alone." See section 48, "The Narratives of Pain."

78. Notes from a Doctor Who Is Much Smarter Than I

In his book *The Biology of Desire,* Dr. Lewis takes a human approach to the problem of addiction. He doesn't paint in shades of guilt and shame, doesn't use *addiction* in simplistic dualistic terms, perhaps because he's fought his own drug and alcohol demons. Now, through his work, he shines a light on the fact that our addictions aren't diseases to be treated or mental illnesses to be cured. Instead, he shows how they are the result of the brain doing what it is meant to do—help us survive in a cruel and pain-filled world.

In the opening chapter, Dr. Lewis shares a comment from a reader: "I see my past drinking as a behavioral problem, a learned response to dealing (or not dealing) with emotional pain and stress. Once I achieved the excavation of my wounds, I no longer lived with the same anxiety or sense of dread/guilt and shame."[7] It's a vulnerable emotional truth, one Lewis seems to find credible. So perhaps it's possible to remove the chemical hooks by dealing with the underlying pain that triggers the need to use those hooks. But how do those chemical hooks work in the first place? How do they drag us deeper into addiction, attachment, habit, affection, and dependency?

---

7   Marc Lewis, *The Biology of Desire: Why Addiction Is Not a Disease* (New York: Public Affairs, 2015), 16–17.

79. HOW CHEMICAL HOOKS HAPPEN

In his book, Dr. Lewis breaks down the science of addiction, and information junkie that I am, I ate it up. And though I'm not an expert on anatomy and physiology,[8] a rudimentary recasting of Dr. Lewis's work may prove helpful in understanding just how the Stuff of Earth gets its hooks in us. And so, with deference to the neuroscientists and doctors in the room, let's examine three major parts of the brain and one neurotransmitter, all of which are primed to chase pleasure when pain comes knocking.

---

8 For what it's worth, I made an A in my senior AP Anatomy and Physiology class at Southside High School in Fort Smith, Arkansas. For those of you acquainted with Ms. Beland's science classes, this is no small feat.

80. A Grand Tour of the Brain

The Prefrontal Cortex (PFC). The PFC is the most evolved part of the brain, the part used in decision making.

The Striatum. The striatum is the motivational engine of the brain. It sets goals for the body, motivates us to pursue certain outcomes and ends. The striatum pushes us to go, go, go, to achieve no matter the cost.

The Midbrain. The midbrain, which includes the ventral tegmental area, is the part of the brain associated with many body functions, including arousal. Dopamine is produced in the ventral tegmental area.

Dopamine. This neurotransmitter fuels desire and plays a part in instigating, motivating, and rewarding desire. It's often called the feel-good neurotransmitter. Scientists now believe that dopamine doesn't so much produce the whizz-bang of pleasure as it directs our brains' attention to it. The Stuff of Earth produces pleasure, and in the euphoria of that pleasure, you'll find dopamine locking the message in: "This feels good; we should do this more."[9]

---

9 Of course, there are other feel-good chemicals released along with dopamine, and which also induce a sort of whizz-bang feeling. These chemicals include endorphins (which heroin mimics), serotonin (which is released after a big meal), and the "cuddle hormone" oxytocin (which is released during sex).

81. THE BRAIN IN PAIN

In any moment of pain or distress, even minor pains like hunger, these parts of the brain (along with scores of others)[10] work together to chase the reward of satisfaction. For this reason, neuroscientists refer to these parts of the brain as the reward center, which, as no small aside, sounds like a location at the retirement village where your grandmother might go to collect her bingo winnings.

How does the reward center work? Consider two hypotheticals.

---

10 Two of the parts of the brain associated with the reward network are the ventral tegmental area and the amygdala. The ventral tegmental area is responsible for releasing dopamine into the body. The amygdala, which my therapist once described as the center of emotional memory, often connects emotion with some need, thus revving up the reward center of the brain. The inner workings of the system are complicated and the subject of much longer books, like *The Biology of Desire*. I'm giving a truncated layman's view in this book for two reasons: (1) I am no medical doctor, though I once dissected the brain of some mammal in high school (which mammal, I cannot recall); (2) others have written astounding explanations of the brain's reward center and how it animates desire and addiction, such as Lewis's *The Biology of Desire*. You can find out more about Lewis's books (and all the other books cited in this work) at sethhaines.com/wakeup.

82. YOUR REWARD CENTER ON FOOD

It's the noon hour on a busy day, a day when you've skipped breakfast out of necessity. You're hard at the grind when your stomach rumbles. A man in the office comes from the break room, walks past your cubicle with a steaming bowl of soup. The rich scent of chicken broth reaches into your work space, tickles your nose, and within a millisecond, your brain gets to work.

Recognizing the body's hunger, the midbrain takes the simple cue (the smell of soup) and dumps dopamine into your brain. The dopamine makes its way to the striatum, provides the fuel to rev up the body's motivational engine. Fully fueled, the striatum sends signals to the PFC: *Do what it takes; come up with a plan; but whatever you do, get this body some food on the double.* The PFC, rational as it is, takes this signal, interprets it, agrees that, *Yeah, we really are hungry and I should reach out to the body's motor neurons to move us out of this cubicle, toward the break room, and to the brown bag we packed before work.* And before you can form any objection to the plan, you're up and out of your cubicle. You're at the refrigerator, pulling out your brown bag. You're back at your desk, unpacking your lunch. You're taking the first bite of your sandwich, and as the flavors mingle on your palate, the brain dumps another load of satisfying chemicals into your system, including a euphoria-inducing dose of dopamine.

Whizz-bang.

The euphoric release of dopamine sends a signal to the striatum, reinforcing its initial message. *See? I told you a little food would fix the hunger pangs.*

This is your reward center on food.

83. YOUR REWARD CENTER ON BOOZE

It's the nine-o'clock hour on a shaky day, a day when you've skipped your nightly toddy because you're trying to cut back. You're at home, nerves on fire, three days into a dry season, and the phone rings. It's your boss and he's so sorry, but he wonders whether you could come in and help drive the Great Big Project across the finish line. You agree, and as you hang up, your stomach knots. Your shoulders pinch up toward your ears.

Your body bears a memory, try as you might to shake it. Perceiving the stress, the reward center remembers the way you've taken the edge off for all those years—whiskey. It spins up before you can formulate a thought. It takes the stress cue, the cue of pain, and it dumps dopamine, the motivational fuel, into your brain. That dopamine makes its way to the striatum, whose memory is well grooved: *In times of stress, alcohol dulls it all.* The striatum does what it's designed to do, sending signals to the PFC: *Find booze; get booze; drink booze.* The PFC, rational as it is, takes this signal, interprets it, but says, *Wait, is this really the best decision? Aren't we trying to cut back?* The midbrain takes its cue, dumps more dopamine into the system, amplifies the striatum's motivational speech: *FIND BOOZE; GET BOOZE; DRINK BOOZE!*

To make matters worse, the reward center begins amplifying emotional messages sent by the amygdala, which serves as the emotional storehouse of the brain. If you don't take the edge off, you might not be able to perform. If you can't perform, you might lose your job. If you lose your job, there won't be enough—money, accolades, whatever. If there's not enough, are you enough?

FIND BOOZE; GET BOOZE; DRINK BOOZE!

The PFC receives the new emotional data, hears the resounding directive, and after years of being trained to silence the voice of pain with booze (just like it was trained to kill hunger with soup), it

123

capitulates. And as you grab your keys and walk out the door, you've already made the decision, or rather your brain has made the decision for you.

There is a liquor store a few miles from the office.

A little nip will take the edge off.

No one will blame you for a little whiskey breath; after all, it's after hours.

After you hit the corner store, after you crack the perforated top of the whiskey bottle, after you take a swig, the brain dumps a load of endorphins and even more dopamine into your system. Within minutes you feel whizz-bang euphoria that reinforces the simple message: *Whiskey dulls the pain even before the buzz sets in.* So you keep drinking until the voices of stress are muted and the body releases even more dopamine into your brain.

This is your reward center on booze.

84. WEAR THAT RECORD OUT

Behind every desire, every reward-seeking behavior, every compulsive habit, you'll find the reward center firing on all cylinders. To be even more specific, you'll find dopamine—the life of the party—doing its thing.

When a heroin addict has a craving, it's the dopamine spike in response to some cue (often sent by the amygdala) that motivates desire for the rush of the chemical high. When he gets his fix, dopamine works in conjunction with synthetic endorphins to bring a satisfying euphoria. In that euphoria, dopamine etches a groove in his brain, creates a record. What tune does the record play?

Heroin brings the fix.

Dopamine is a lackluster composer, though, and it plays the same tune for each of our coping mechanisms, changing a singular lyric. What do I mean?

THE BOOK OF WAKING UP

85. GROOVE 1: MOMMY'S WINE

At the end of a stressful day picking up after her toddler, a mom jumps on Facebook and pronounces, "It's Mommy's Wine Time!" You read the post and before you decide whether you should push the thumbs-up or laugh emoji, the midbrain dumps a load of dopamine into the reward center. You've had a stressful day too. Don't you deserve a glass of wine? You go to the kitchen, pour the chardonnay, take a drink, and as the alcohol begins to wash away the stress of your day, your brain releases more dopamine. It's this dopamine that sings the song: *Alcohol brings the fix.*

86. Groove 2: Meghan Markle's Sweater

You're on the hunt for the perfect cashmere sweater, dopamine fueling the hunt. That sweater—the Everlane variety made famous by Meghan Markle—has been out of stock for weeks, but you check the website and it's available. You add it to the cart, click "Continue to Checkout." Anticipating the reward, your brain dumps another load of dopamine into your system. And as you type in your credit card number, as you anticipate the arrival of your new cashmere sweater, that dopamine reinforces the message—buying stuff feels good—and for the moment, that dopaminergic music drowns out the want, the pain, the stress as it croons, *Buying brings the fix.*

87. GROOVE 3: SEXUAL HEALING

Dopamine surges through the body before a good romp, fuels the message of fixation: *Sex, sex, sex.* When we find that temporal satisfaction, the whizz-bang shot of oxytocin and dopamine etches another groove. Sex silences the want, the pain, the stress, whatever, at least for a few hours.

Hear the music? *Sex brings the fix.*

88. Groove 4: Gustation

When our stomachs rumble, our reward centers rev up in anticipation of good vittles, and there's the dopamine again, firing up the machine. When we satiate that hunger, there's dopamine again, reminding us that food silences the want, the pain, the stress, whatever.

Food brings the fix.

It's not just narcotics, booze, shopping, and sex that work our reward centers over, though. Consider the whizz-bang brought by using any old thing as a coping mechanism. Consider the grooves you'd rather not consider.

89: Groove 5: Social Consumption

What is social media but technological heroin? It's a distracting hook, an attention manipulator, a time suck. It's equal parts feast, famine, fear, ego, and political dumpster fire, and the content (at least the nonadvertisement content) is created by the people for the people. It's *our* method of mass communication, *our* way to be heard, *our* method of connecting with people when we're alone. This centering of our own message, opinion, need, whatever—doesn't it etch a groove?

No matter how much I swear it off, I always end up back on the social-media sauce. Why? When I'm alone, my brain plays the groove in the record: *Media brings the fix.*

Humans were created for social connection. It's that need that drives friendship, marriage, societal harmony. What happens neurologically when we make those social connections? First comes the oxytocin—*whizz-bang*. Then comes a new rush of dopamine, fixing the memory of that whizz-bang firmly in place.

The science behind our attachment to social media is certain. We seek connection—even if a virtual, cotton-candy version of the real—and Facebook, Twitter, Snapchat, Instagram, even LinkedIn facilitate a kind of connection. (Even now, aren't you thinking about social media? Even now, can't you feel the dopamine firing up the striatum, can't you feel the tug toward virtual connection?) Scientists—even the ones working for the social media giants—know that social media primes the flow of dopamine in the brain, dragging us to the reward of this electronic connection. They know that every time we update our statuses, like other people's statuses, or receive a like on our statuses, every time we reap the reward of social media use, our brains release more dopamine, locking the memory of this virtual connection in place.

But it's not just the need for connection that drives our habituated desires toward social media. The social-media giants also use certain psychological tricks to stimulate the release of more dopamine. What are those tricks? Unpredictability, incomplete satisfaction, and the cues of potential rewards.[11] Consider:

Unpredictability: What is social media if not an unpredictable hodgepodge of family photos, angry political banter, adorable cat memes, and touching parenting videos?
Incomplete Satisfaction: Can 280 characters tell the whole story, convey full conversational nuance, or create complete connection?
Cues of Potential Rewards: Don't the notifications, the hums, buzzes, and dings of your cell phone drive you back to social media platforms time and time again?

These features drive the cycles of desire, of want, of fixation, and each time we reach for our cell phones to satisfy the craving, the feel-good chemicals, including dopamine, etch the groove a little deeper: *Social media brings the fix.*

11 Susan Weinschenk, "Why We're All Addicted to Texts, Twitter, and Google," *Psychology Today*, September 11, 2012, https://www.psychologytoday.com/us/blog/brain-wise/201209/why-were-all-addicted-texts-twitter-and-google.

90. Groove 6: Vegas, Baby

Some of the cues that prime the dopamine pump during social media use—unpredictability, incomplete satisfaction, and the cues of potential rewards—fuel other reward-seeking behaviors too. Consider your brain on gambling.

> *Unpredictability:* Pull the lever and watch the images spin; wonder whether they'll come up three cherries.
>
> *Incomplete Satisfaction:* The machine does what the machine does, but three cherries is not your lot. Still, it's an incremental win. A buck or two. Enough to reinforce the notion that, yes, there really are rewards locked in this puzzle box. What's the chemical reinforcing that notion? Dopamine.
>
> *Cues of Potential Rewards:* The woman at the machine next to you lets out a little squeal of excitement. She's won a couple hundred, maybe more. If she can do it, can't you?

What's more, it's that flow of dopamine that drives our desire to chase returns when we're down on our luck at a slot machine or seated at the blackjack table.[12] Dopamine—he's the slave driver, and we do what it takes to honor our debt to him.

---

12 Chris Baraniuk, "Why Gamblers Get High Even When They Lose," BBC, July 21, 2016, http://www.bbc.com/future/story/20160721-the-buzz-that-keeps-people-gambling.

91. GROOVE 7: BODY SURFING

We're all adults here. Let's watch porn work. (Which is not to say let's watch porn.)

> *Unpredictability:* Click the link and what do you get? Infinite bodies. Infinite possibilities.
>
> *Cues of Potential Rewards:* What is porn if not the personification of potential reward?
>
> *Incomplete Satisfaction:* How much communion or connection is there through a screen? Sure you get that whizz-bang cocktail of norepinephrine, endorphins, oxytocin, and dopamine if you take porn use all the way to the logical conclusion. But how long does that whizz-bang rush last before the guilt sets in?

In a world of instant access and instant gratification, our dopamine pumps are primed by the prospect of virtual satisfaction, particularly sexual satisfaction. What's more, the spigots of those pumps are opened wide by the unpredictability, partial satisfaction, and reward cues that keep us chasing the mystery locked in another night of naked bodies.

92. GROOVES 8, 9, 10, 11, 12, *ETCETERA, AD NAUSEAM*

The brain's reward center, which includes the production and release of dopamine, pushes us toward both making and spending money, playing video games,[13] use or overuse of the internet,[14] and consumption (even binge consumption) of the latest Netflix series.[15] Dopamine even spikes when you hear the hook to your favorite Beyoncé jam on your bumper-to-bumper morning commute. Yes, pop music produces almost addictive brain chemistry.[16] Every compulsive thing works on the same neurological systems. And though different whizz-bang chemicals might be involved in sex, drugs, and rock-and-roll, one neurotransmitter is common—dopamine. It's the neurotransmitter that locks the memory of the whizz-bang in place, that drives our desire.

Again.

And again.

And again.

Priming us for more, more, more.

---

13 David J. Linden, "Video Games Can Activate the Brain's Pleasure Circuits," *Psychology Today*, October 25, 2011, https://www.psychologytoday.com/us/blog/the-compass-pleasure/201110/video-games-can-activate-the-brains-pleasure-circuits-0.

14 Bill Davidow, "Exploring the Neuroscience of Internet Addiction," *The Atlantic*, July 18, 2012, https://www.theatlantic.com/health/archive/2012/07/exploiting-the-neuroscience-of-internet-addiction/259820/.

15 Dr. Renee Carr, a clinical psychologist, says it's because of the chemicals being released in our brains. "When engaged in an activity that's enjoyable such as binge watching, your brain produces dopamine," she explains. "This chemical gives the body a natural, internal reward of pleasure that reinforces continued engagement in that activity. It is the brain's signal that communicates to the body, 'This feels good. You should keep doing this!' When binge watching your favorite show, your brain is producing dopamine, and your body experiences a drug-like high. You experience a pseudo-addiction to the show because you develop cravings for dopamine."

16 Sara G. Miller, "Your Brain on Music: Why Certain Songs Bring Pleasure," *Live Science*, February 8, 2017, https://www.livescience.com/57789-music-brain-opioids.html.

93. OUR SECOND BRIEF PAUSE TO REFLECT

Pause. Breathe. Take another moment to reflect on addiction. Can you name the grooves in your life, the coping mechanisms that have been reinforced by years of dopamine stimulation? If not, use the cliche acronym HALT as your rubric for identifying them. You've heard this, haven't you?

- When you're hungry, what food do you turn to?
- When you're angry, what do you reach for to douse the fire?
- When you're lonely, how do you find relief? What do you click?
- When you're tired, what bad habit, vice, or compulsion do you fall into?

When all four of these states of being come crashing down on you at once, what coping mechanism can't you refuse, what compulsion drags you down? If you turn to the Stuff of Earth when you're hungry, angry, lonely, or tired, or all four, there's a good chance you're running in a groove etched by a dopamine loop.

94. DON'T PICK ON DOPAMINE

Disclaimer: Our brain chemistry is not broken or sinful or whatever. The fact that our brains react to cues, that they seek satisfying pleasures during seasons of stress or pain or want, is simple biology. God created us with this brain chemistry, and when we're awake to this truth, we see how the pleasures of sex, food, wine, even painkillers lead us deeper into the recognition of the goodness of God in the land of the living (Ps. 27:13).

God being God, he could have designed us to have a much less complicated system, I suppose. He could have created a world without pleasures, could have equipped us with a series of egg timers attached to our bodies, each labeled with some sort of action.

Ding—eat.

Ding—drink.

Ding—make money.

Ding—entertain.

Ding—have sex.

He could have created us without any needs. He could have created a world in which there was no need to partner with him in satisfying those needs.

What a boring world that would be.

95. THE HIJACKING

What God intended for good, though, has a couple of drawbacks.

Drawback 1: When we get too acquainted with the lyrics of any one tune—*Food brings the fix; buying brings the fix; sex brings the fix*—we can't quit playing the record. Those grooves become etched so deeply that we try to use the tune to silence any pain. (For instance, I used booze to fix work stress, health stress, family stress, the stress of almost dismembering my thumb chopping onions.)

Drawback 2: The powers of the world know our propensity to sing the same songs over and over again, and they encourage it. Beer makers, video game creators, and meth cookers all use our brain chemistry against us, peddling various coping mechanisms to line their pocketbooks. (If you don't believe me, take inventory of next year's Super Bowl ads. What are they but promises of the whizz-bang associated with products?) But as one of those kooky religious types, I'm by-God convinced that these industry powers are motivated by darker, sneakier spiritual powers. Recall Screwtape's twisting of the pleasures? What is his twisting but an attempt to encourage coping mechanisms? Screwtape and his ilk (the powers) want nothing more than to steal our hard-earned cash, kill our willpower, and destroy our connection with God by using the Stuff of Earth—the stuff created by God—as a distraction to keep us alienated from God.[17] The powers won't stop, either, not until we offer homage to the Stuff of Earth, not until we're completely attached to them.

---

17 For a holistic look at the powers, pick up a copy of Marva Dawn's book *Powers, Weakness, and the Tabernacling of God*. In that book, she shows how the powers are much more than the impish demons of our limited imaginations. The powers include demonic forces, she says, but also the systems of the world, like commerce, politics, education, and the like.

96. The Modern Ingredients of Addiction

The powers are ever at work, and in this modern economy, they have more tools at their disposal to drive addictions (perhaps even superaddictions). They have corporations, ad agencies, multilevel marketing schemes, gymnasiums, publishers, governments, and all manner of man-made things at their disposal. They have more intoxicating ingredients too—more fats, hyperconcentrated sugars, synthetic opioids, bodies, whatever. In the modern era, the powers can put us on an endless dopamine-fueled rollercoaster, the kind of rollercoaster that didn't exist in eras past.

Hungry? Reach for a box of cookies, a box you chose from among dozens at the store. Take, eat. Three minutes in, you've consumed a day's worth of calories for someone living in the eighteenth century. And there it is, the whizz-bang.

Yeah, that's the stuff.

Are your jeans a little threadbare? Jump on the internet. Visit the Gap, Banana Republic, Everlane. Options, options, options—so many mind-numbing options. An hour later, you've narrowed it down to three pair, and you buy them all, check out with the credit-card information stored on your computer. What would have taken a half-day outing just thirty years ago was all done from the well-worn divot in your favorite living-room chair.

Whizz-bang.

Feeling that itch? You know the one. Click and scroll, click and scroll. Ten bodies. Hundreds of bodies. Endless options of bodies. All these options birthed by technology. How is it even possible?

Whizz-bang.
Whizz-bang.
Whizz-bang.

97. THE EASE OF EXCESS PLEASURES

See how it works? Our brain chemistry pushes us to meet certain needs, to cure certain stresses and pain points, to scratch certain itches. And though people were subject to addictions in days past, there's a subtle difference in today's society. In days past, humans had to work harder to attain excess pleasures. Was there access to such calorically dense foods, so many clothing options, the ability to choose from hundreds of sexual partners a night?

I'm no expert in the history of addictions, but I know a good deal about modern Western society, and it doesn't take much to see the ways the powers (and their people) use excess to fuel our addictions.

Food companies know that more sugar drives more desire, leading to more consumption.

Retail companies know that more options drives more desire, leading to more purchases.

Entertainment companies know that more naked bodies drives desire, bringing more viewers to the tube.

Social media companies know that more digital connection, more likes and comments and retweets drives desire, brings more attention to their platform.

Each of these industries knows something else too. Driving desire leads to more money, the stuff the industry powers desire more than anything.[18]

The powers know their game, and they attach a line straight to the reward centers of our brains, give us a pump button to push anytime we feel the call of desire. Asleep as we are to the powers at

---

18 During the writing of this book, I discovered that 20 percent of the content I consumed on Instagram and 12.5 percent of the content I consumed on Facebook and Twitter were targeted advertisements. For more on this discovery, visit sethhaines.com/wakeup and watch "Social Media: The Profit of Addiction."

work, numbed as we are by the whizz-bang of pleasures, we don't pull the line out. Over time, we begin pushing the button to numb again and again in an attempt to satisfy deeper desires. Meanwhile, the chemical hooks sink in more deeply.

98. SO IS ADDICTION A DISEASE?

Dr. Lewis makes no mention of the powers in his work, and I wouldn't expect him to. As far as I know, he's not a religious kook like I am. He knows how our coping mechanisms, our habits, addictions, and dependencies, are influenced by the brain chemistry of desire, though, chemistry that's influenced by myriad factors in the world around us. What's more, he knows that addictions can form to any number of behaviors. He writes,

> One of the greatest blows to the current notion of addiction as a disease is the fact that behavioral addictions can be just as severe as substance addictions. The party line of NIDA, the AMA, and the American Society of Addiction Medicine remains what it has been for decades: addiction is primarily caused by substance abuse. But if that were so, why are addictions to porn, sex, internet games, food, and gambling so ubiquitous? And why do "disorders" characterized by too much of any of the above show brain activities nearly identical to those shown in drug addiction?[19]

All of us really can be addicted to something. But it's not just Dr. Lewis who believes that nonchemical behavioral addictions are possible. Dr. Vivek Murthy, former United States Surgeon General, agrees. In an interview with *National Geographic,* he indicated that addiction is "characterized not necessarily by dependence or withdrawal but by compulsive repetition of an activity despite life-damaging consequences. This view has led many scientists to accept

---

19 Lewis, *Biology of Desire,* 165.

the once heretical idea that addiction is possible without drugs."[20] So compulsive shopping (with its life-damaging consequences to your pocketbook), compulsive gaming (with its life-damaging consequences to your grade point average), compulsive eating (with its life-damaging consequences to your life) can all be addictions. Any pleasure can be turned by the powers into a coping mechanism.

20 Fran Smith, "How Science Is Unlocking the Secrets of Addiction," *National Geographic*, September 2017, https://www.nationalgeographic.com/magazine/2017/09/the-addicted-brain/.

99. A POP QUIZ

"So what is the connection between addictions (both chemical and behavioral) and pain?" you might be asking. A worthy question, but before we tackle it, how about a pop quiz for review?

DIRECTIONS: FOR EACH STATEMENT,
CIRCLE TRUE OR FALSE.

T or F: We all experience pain.
T or F: We all have a reward center, a system which motivates us to relieve some stress, some need, some pain.
T or F: The pleasures produced by the reward center are sacramental, meant to point us to the God who created those pleasures.
T or F: The powers (both natural and spiritual) do everything they can to hijack our reward centers to point us to created objects instead of to the God who created them.

BONUS QUESTION

T or F: You've experienced your own hijacking.

If you answered false to any of these questions, take the test again. (This is a pass-fail test.) If you answered true to each of these questions, and if you answered the bonus question correctly, ask yourself, "What motivates and animates my uncontrollable desires?"

100. The Nexus between Pain and Gin

Before my son's sickness, before I was faced with my darkest season of struggle, my brain learned the ways alcohol takes the edge off a stressful day. So as the stress of the average workday gave way to the pain of my son's sickness, as I sensed the scarcity of faith, healing, and the presence of God, my brain suggested a time-tested remedy.

My brain said, "If liquor numbs the everyday stress of work, maybe it'll numb the pain of scarcity."

I took the message, rolled it over again and again, and decided (subconsciously, of course) that yes, booze might numb this pain, and so I gave it a shot. One drink worked pretty well. Two drinks worked better. Three was the magic number, at least for a few weeks. Then it was four. Maybe five. Night after night, I pickled my pain. Night after night, my reward center responded, digging a deep groove of dependency, addiction, or habit.

My brain said, "Yes, booze works to silence narratives of scarcity, even if it pulls you to hazy sleep."

101. Quitting Can't Make the Pain Go Away, So Quitting Doesn't Fix Everything

After the epiphany in the Methodist church lobby, after ninety days of therapy, I came to see how what had once been a harmless stress-management mechanism (the five-o'clock cocktail) had become an anesthetizing agent. Booze silenced the stress of work, so wouldn't it silence the stress of my sick child? Even if it took more than a double? Or a triple? Or a liter?

When I walked away from the bottle, I suppose I thought that meant I was sober. But even though I'd quit drinking, I still had to face the pain of my son's sickness, and my brain, now booze free, looked for other anesthetizing agents, other ways to kill the pain—sex, chocolate, book buying, work. Even as I invited God into my pain, even as I began to feel peace and something like healing, I still sensed the pull to other coping mechanisms, other anesthesia. I saw the way food, commerce, materialism, and entertainment called to me, how they promised to pull me from my pain.[21]

---

21 In *Coming Clean*, I wrote it this way: "Commerce, materialism, entertainment, the endless chase of perfection—aren't these also ways to avoid the restlessness rattling in our bones? Aren't these just another way to numb? Aren't these another sleight of hand? We become entranced people, zombies longing for the Stuff of Earth without thought of the truest perfect—the unity of home."

102. THE LITERATURE OF PAIN

I'm an experiential expert, a walking set of emotional data whose journey supports this point: Pain is the horse that pulls the cart of addiction. It's the coal that fires the steam engine. It's the power behind the power, the thing that pulls the thing, the force producing the force.

I'm not alone in my expertise, though. I've reads scores of poems, hundreds of stories, watched endless hours of addiction films, and time and time again, there is one common truth: humans use addictions, habits, and dependencies to numb the pains of life. Consider a few examples.

In *Confessions of an English Opium Eater*, Thomas De Quincey writes, "Oh, just, subtle, and all-conquering opium! . . . [T]hat, to the hearts of rich and poor alike, for the wounds that will never heal, and for the pangs of grief that 'tempt the spirit to rebel,' bringest an assuaging balm."[22]

In *Lit*, poet and recovering booze-hound Mary Karr writes, "What hurts so bad about youth isn't the actual butt whippings the world delivers. It's the stupid hopes playacting like certainties."[23]

In *Between Breaths*, journalist and alcoholic Elizabeth Vargas writes, "When fear is your default state of mind, you try very hard to control everything. It is a futile battle that can leave you exhausted, and desperate for relief."[24]

---

22 Thomas De Quincey, *Confessions of an English Opium Eater* (Edinburgh: Adam and Charles Black, 1862), 212.

23 Mary Karr, *Lit* (New York: HarperLuxe, 2009), 29.

24 Elizabeth Vargas, *Between Breaths: A Memoir of Panic and Addiction* (New York: Grand Central Publishing, 2016).

103. BEGINNING IN PAIN

Maybe the musings of poets and journalists aren't convincing to you. Maybe you'd be more convinced by comedian and pop-culture icon of addiction Russell Brand, who says in an interview with the *New York Times*, "We are trying to solve inner problems externally—whatever it is in our lives that is missing. . . . Eckhart Tolle said it perfectly: 'Addiction starts with pain and ends with pain.'"[25]

25 Judith Newman, "Recovery, Russell Brand Style," *New York Times*, October 16, 2017, https://www.nytimes.com/2017/10/16/books/russell-brand-addiction-recovery.html.

THE BOOK OF WAKING UP

104. Asking the Right Question

If literary figures and comedians aren't enough proof, consider the scientists who agree with De Quincey, Karr, Vargas, Brand, and me. Dr. Gabor Maté writes, "Addictions always originate in pain, whether felt openly or hidden in the unconscious. They are emotional anesthetics." Put more succinctly, he writes, "The question is never 'Why the addiction?' but 'Why the pain?'"

105. NUMBING OURSELVES TO SLEEP

If it's true that pain drives addiction, and if we're all subject to the pains of life—didn't Jesus himself say, "In this life you will have pain"?[26]—then doesn't it stand to reason that all of us might use the whizz-bang pleasures of the Stuff of Earth to numb or dull that pain? Couldn't it be that we are all drunk on something? And couldn't it also be that we're all asleep to the various ways we medicate?

---

26 My artistic paraphrase of John 16:33.

106. Another Pause to Examine the Fix

Consider that coping mechanism you just can't shake. Consider that song that burrows into your subconscious like an earworm: *This is the fix; this is the fix; this is the fix.* In the quietness of this space, pen in hand, examine your life. The fix—what pain is it trying to address? Consider, for example, the substitutionary fix I can't seem to shake—buying books. Why do I keep buying and buying and buying?

If I find the right book, I'll have access to the right knowledge.

If I acquire the right knowledge, perhaps then I'll have enough, know enough, be enough.

If I have enough, know enough, am enough, perhaps then I'll be able to silence scarcity narratives.

Now it's your turn. What pain narratives are you trying to silence with your coping mechanisms?

107. The Big Picture of Pain and Addiction

Let's review.

Heroin. Booze. Boobs. Slot machines. Shopping. Eating. In all cases, dopamine fuels desire, ignites the striatum to fixate on that desire, to motivate the PFC to chart a course to the X on the treasure map. We learn that these pleasures relieve stress and numb certain pains. And as the writers, comedians, scientists, and I have all noted, we can attempt to use these pleasures to silence the pain narratives. But if there's one thing we've all learned, it's this: those pleasures can never cure the pain. Not really. They're only temporary anesthetics, and when we come out from under their effects, we're left with a fierce hunger for more relief.

Perhaps this accounts for Russell Brand's likening his various addictions—whether to drugs, alcohol, food, or fame—to a "tumultuous ever restless cosmic force of deranged appetites . . . trying to devour the galaxy and its planets." In the end, though, he recognized the truth behind every addiction. Addiction is nothing more than attachment to the thing that can never satisfy our deepest longing, the longing for bonded connection. In an interview with an Australian news program, he says, "It doesn't matter if you're addicted to sex or drugs or codependent relationships. What matters is there's a yearning within in you, and I think it's in all of us, a yearning for connection. And if that yearning isn't correctly directed, it will *attach* like some mad duckling following a tractor to whatever external stimuli is present"[27] (emphasis added).

27 Russell Brand, "Deranged Appetites," Australian TV interview, October 2017, https://www.youtube.com/watch?v=hKR3nt5Cw-M.

108. THE ATTACHMENTS THAT RULE OUR LIVES

Brand isn't the only one who's likened addiction to a misplaced attachment. In his book *Addiction and Grace*, psychiatrist Gerald May explores the causes and effects of addiction, taking a whole-human approach in his work. Making good use of psychology, brain chemistry, and Christian theology, May shows how desire is the catalyst for addiction. He writes, "I have now come to believe that addiction is a separate and even more self-defeating force that abuses our freedom and makes us do things we really do not want to do. While repression stifles desire, addiction attaches desire, bonds and enslaves the energy of desire to certain specific behaviors, things, or people. These objects of attachment then become preoccupations and obsessions; they come to rule our lives."[28]

---

28 Gerald G. May, *Addiction and Grace: Love and Spirituality in the Healing of Addictions* (New York: Harper Collins, 1998), 14.

109. The Concept of Attachment in the Christian Tradition

The idea of addictions being nothing more than attachments to things—drugs, alcohol, food, money, gambling, gaming, sex, whatever—is not the offspring of pop psychology and religion. It's a concept rooted in one of Christianity's most famous works on spiritual formation, *The Spiritual Exercises* of St. Ignatius of Loyola.

Ignatius, the sixteenth-century Spanish theologian who founded the Society of Jesus (or the Jesuits), wasn't always a spiritual guru. Ignatius described himself before his conversion to Christianity as "a man given to the vanities of the world, whose chief delight consisted in martial exercises, with a great and vain desire to win renown." He was a glory hound, a man attached to the notion that fame, power, and perhaps wealth would satisfy his own deranged appetites. Fame and glory wouldn't be his fate, though. After a battlefield injury and the resulting surgery, Ignatius was laid up in a castle, one with poor wifi connection (like most castles in the sixteenth century) and a spartan library boasting only two books, one about the life of Christ and one about the lives of the saints. He consumed the books, and as he did, his ambitions turned to purer pursuits—the pursuit of the devout life.

After his recovery, Ignatius nursed a deep affection for Christ. He attended daily mass, tempered his appetites for food, drink, and material wealth. And though he spent hours a day in prayer, often cloistering himself in a cave outside of town, and though he lived a life of strict discipline, he hoped to provide a way for the common man. He wanted to pave a road for his people—for you and me—a road we could walk straight into Divine Love.

110. The *Exercises*: A Way of Proper Attachment

Ignatius knew by experience the power of attachments. Attachments to glory, fame, and money—his coping mechanisms—motivated him before his conversion. Attachment to Christ motivated him after. Recognizing these two seasons, and knowing the power of attachment to Christ, he wrote the *Exercises*. What is the purpose of the *Exercises?* Ignatius writes it this way:

The Purpose: "[W]e call Spiritual Exercises every way of preparing and disposing the soul to rid itself of all inordinate attachments, and, after their removal, of seeking and finding the will of God in the disposition of our life for the salvation of our soul."[29]

Huh?

I'd offer this paraphrase.

A Purpose Paraphrase: "The purpose of the *Exercises* is to cut away things that drag us away from God, and instead to attach to God."

---

29 A complete translation of *The Spiritual Exercises* by Louis J. Puhl, SJ, can be found at http://spex.ignatianspirituality.com/SpiritualExercises/Puhl.

111. ON ATTACHMENT AS A WORD

Admission: I understand what Brand, May, and the good St. Ignatius are saying. I know how the Stuff of Earth gets its hooks in us, how our coping mechanisms come to feel like attachments dragging us around by the hooks. But does the term *attachment* resonate with you, especially when used in a phrase like Ignatius's *inordinate attachment*? Doesn't it have a clinical ring to it?

I'm no Spaniard, nor am I a linguist. My understanding of the Spanish language is less than none. But in Ignatius's native pen, the word rendered as attachment is the word *afección*. (*Afección*—now there's a sexier, more invigorating word.) The word *afección* conjures images of deep love, doesn't it? In this light, perhaps I could offer a better paraphrase of the purpose of the *Exercises*.

A Better Purpose Paraphrase: "The purpose of the *Exercises* is to break up with the lesser loves the world offers and fall into mad *afección* with God."

112. MISPLACED ADORATION

Over the years, theologians, priests, pastors, and spiritual directors have preached, written, and opined about what constitutes a disordered attachment, an *afección* we place over our desire for divine *afección*.[30] I might sum up much of that opinion this way: when we enter into a long-term relationship with a coping mechanism in an attempt to silence a narrative of pain or to numb ourselves to it or to distract ourselves from it, we're nursing an affection for lesser loves. We're adoring the creation instead of the Creator.

Addiction: What is it but misplaced adoration?

---

30 In an interview with Krista Tippett, Father James Martin, SJ, discusses the purpose of the *Exercises*. Consider this brief excerpt from that interview.

"Ms. Tippett: Tell me what you mean when you say and when you write, 'The way of Ignatius was about finding freedom.' How are you using that word?

"Fr. Martin: Well, Ignatius wanted us to be free of anything that kept us from following God. He called them disordered attachments. And the idea is that if anything keeps you from being more open to God's will in your life, get rid of it, basically."

See Krista Tippett, "James Martin: Finding God in All Things," *On Being, with Krista Tippett*, December 18, 2014, https://onbeing.org/programs/james-martin-finding-god-in-all -things-2/.

113. ADDICTION AS SLEEP

In the Scriptures, drunkenness, addiction, attachment, disordered *afección*, misplaced adoration—whatever you want to call it—is likened to sleep. In his first letter to the Thessalonians, Paul asks the congregation to control their bodies, their desires, their lusts. Calling them "children of light," he encourages them not to "fall asleep as others do, but let us keep awake and be sober" (1 Thess. 5:5–6 NRSV). In his letter to the Romans, he gives similar encouragement, asking the people to stop indulging every drunken, greedy, sexual desire and to "wake from sleep" (Rom. 13:11–14 ESV). In his letter to the Ephesians, he writes, "Awake, O sleeper" (5:14 ESV), implying that drunkenness and debauchery (such a good-old-fashioned southern-church-lady word) make us drowsy.

See? As we turn to lesser loves for relief, as we adore them, as we attach ourselves to the fleeting comfort they bring, they lull us to sleep with a siren's lullaby.

What Is Sobriety?

I love You and desire You. Come into my heart. . . . Absorb my mind that I may die through love of Your love.

—St. Francis of Assisi

We're not meant to wallow in pleasure. Pleasure is joy's assassin.

—Mary Karr, *Lit*

114. WHAT DOES IT MEAN TO LIVE AWAKE?

If turning to coping mechanisms or nursing our bad habits, addictions, dependencies, and disordered attachments is akin to falling asleep, and if sobriety is waking up, then what does it mean to live awake? Really awake?

To lay the groundwork, ask yourself this question: Is waking into sobriety always as simple as quitting some act? Maybe it is. But maybe it's not. Consider Alex.

Alex lives in Oklahoma or California or Montana, and has a husband or a wife or three kids or a dog. She is a stay-at-home mom. He is a hard-charging pastor. Alex, now thirty-five, has wrestled with an eating disorder since high school.

An Alex who knows me called, said she'd heard I'd quit drinking. "Good for you," she said, but then followed with, "You realize you're the luckiest son of a bitch in the room, right?" It was an odd comment, one I hadn't heard in my six-month stint into sobriety, and unsure what to say, I didn't fill the space between our phones with words. I just stood in my kitchen staring at the sink, blinking dumbly.

Alex let the awkward silence hang. (She enjoys a dramatic pause.) She apologized for the profanity and pushed into an explanation. "You drink too much, which is hard, I'm sure," she said, "but you can just quit. I have an eating disorder. I can't just quit eating—that's my problem—but I can't exactly eat all the time either because that would trigger the old wounds. It's a sort of metaphorical pickle."

115. WHY THE ADDICTION, ALEX?

Alex after Alex has told me of her or his struggle to maintain sobriety when it comes to food, and on nearly every occasion, there's some pain underlying the struggle.

Alex No. 1: Alex eats, goes to the full-length mirror, checks her thighs, her abs. She remembers her father asking her what she's been doing to stay in shape, and that's when the brain catches fire, and looking at her reflection again, she wonders whether her thigh gap is a centimeter wider than it was yesterday. She wonders whether she should skip dinner tonight, maybe breakfast tomorrow. While she's at it, maybe she should fast for a few days, maybe run an extra mile. If she could lose another centimeter, wouldn't that kill the memories?

Alex No. 2: After dinner, Alex hears the whispers of his molester. He remembers the days of abuse, recalls how his low self-esteem and bad body image made him easy prey. He can't stop the cascade of thoughts, and before he can think, he reaches for his belly, pinches to the sides of his belly button. His brain catches fire. He can't control what happened in the past, but he can control his weight. As Alex packs his gym bag, he decides to skip his morning meal. Somehow this brings relief.

For the Alexes, food triggers old narratives of pain, and that's when desire sets in. To starve. To binge eat. To barf. To work out a little extra. To do whatever it takes to achieve the whizz-bang feeling of control over food or the body. They walk the tightrope of not enough or too much, and no matter which option they choose, neither eating nor abstinence alone brings a sense of centered sobriety.

See? To eat or not to eat? That is not the question.

Because the question of sobriety goes far beyond our behavior.

THE BOOK OF WAKING UP

116. Sneaky, Sleepy Transfer Addictions

"Sure," you might say, "sobriety means a different thing when you're talking about food. But with drugs and alcohol, quitting makes you sober. Right?"

Maybe. Maybe not.

In her article "Off the Drugs, Onto the Cupcakes," Abby Ellin shares the story of Rodney Zimmerman, who was down to a gaunt 135 pounds when he kicked his heroin habit.[1] While in rehab, he ate a high-calorie, high-fat, trash-food diet, and when he reentered the real world, he continued eating this way. Three years later, Zimmerman was reported to be 250 pounds.

According to the article, Zimmerman says, "I learned how to be sober, but I didn't learn how to take care of all of me."

Sober? Really?

Zimmerman's language shows just how narrowly tailored the word *sober* is these days. We use it to mean a certain thing: not doing addiction X. But gaining 115 pounds in three years as a result of eating sugar and fat—does this sound like something a sober person does?

Because sugary foods have similar effects on the brain as some drugs and alcohol, scientists have noted the prevalence of "transfer addictions" in substance abusers. In her article, Ellin interviewed Christopher Kennedy Lawford, author of *What Addicts Know*, who says, "When you're used to shooting heroin or drinking a bottle of vodka, sugar seems really benign. It's hard to take it seriously. . . . You can't get an addict into recovery until you deal with every aspect of their life. . . . What you think, how you think, how you relate to people,

---

1 Abby Ellin, "Off the Drugs, Onto the Cupcakes," *Well* (blog), *New York Times*, August 15, 2014, https://well.blogs.nytimes.com/2014/09/15/addiction-recovery-weight-gain-nutrition.

what you put in your body, how you exercise—it's all related. And we need to get smarter about it."

Lawford knows the truth: Without dealing with the underlying issues of dependency (what you think, how you think, why you think), we'll move from one sleep-inducing addiction to the next, even if the next is more socially acceptable. Without an approach to dependency that treats the whole person, including the underlying narratives of pain, we'll never walk in waking sobriety.

117. It's All about Ordering Our Loves

To be sober—what does it mean but to be awake to *all* our coping mechanisms, even our transfer addictions? What is true sobriety if not ensuring that we're seeking God for the things only he can give and that we're using the pleasures of the world as he intended. This is the message of the Scriptures: Love the Lord your God first; love your neighbor as much as you love yourself—and by implication, love everything else under that (Matt. 22:37–38). Sobriety is all about ordering our affections, our loves. It's about being awake to God in every moment, even the moments of our pain, and fixing our adoration to him. It's a call that can be seen throughout the Scriptures, even in the oft-misunderstood Ten Commandments. Don't believe me?

118. The Commandments of *Afección*

Consider the Ten Commandments of the Old Testament. What are they but ways of training us to love God first, our neighbors second, and everything else last? What are they but ways of reminding us to adore the Creator over the created? Consider each commandment.

Commandment 1: Don't have any gods before me.

Or, Love me first.

Commandment 2: Don't bow in worship to any created thing.

Or, Love and adore the Creator above the creation.

Commandment 3: Don't misuse the name of the Lord your God.

Or, Value the name of Divine Love above your love of language.

Commandment 4: Remember the Sabbath and don't work on it.

Or, Adore me more than the tasks I've given you to do.

Commandment 5: Honor your pops and your mom.

Or, Practice Divine Love in the context of your family.

Commandment 6: Don't kill.

Or, Participate with me in Divine Love by honoring the life of others created by God.

Commandment 7: Don't sleep with another man's wife.

Or, Allow your love for me to supersede your sexual desires.

Commandment 8: Don't steal.

Or, Allow your love for me to supersede your want for your neighbor's goods.

Commandment 9: Don't lie.

Or, Allow your love for me to supersede your penchant for shading the truth to make yourself look better or get yourself out of trouble or whatever.

Commandment 10: Don't want someone else's stuff.

Or, See commandments 7 and 8 and apply the lessons of Divine Love found therein.

Sure, the commandments contain a healthy dose of dos (do remember the Sabbath; do honor your folks) and do-nots (the rest of them), but there's a singular message behind each: learn the way of elevating God and others above your desires. Or in the words of St. Ignatius, learn the way of divine *afección*.

Examine those commandments again. If it were possible to live them out perfectly, wouldn't we be free from those coping mechanisms we can't seem to shake? Wouldn't we be ever awake to God's love for us?

119. A LITTLE HELP FROM OUR FRIEND

If the commandments do anything, they remind us just how hard-headed we are. We break the rules, eat the forbidden fruit. We still dance before golden calves and sacrifice our time and talents on the altars of lesser gods. We ignore God's love, follow our hungers to things that won't satisfy, all the while chanting, "Make Appetites Great Again."

Even the best rule-followers of biblical times missed the point of the commandments. They extrapolated, made laws around the laws in an attempt to keep themselves pure. But even these well-meaning attempts to keep from screwing it all up were just another way to adore the creation (their laws) over the Creator. They treated the law as the end, not the means for being drawn deeper into the Divine Love.

I don't suspect any of this caught God off guard. He knew we'd miss the point, and after allowing us sufficient time to realize our boneheadedness, the God of smoke and fire shape-shifted and came to earth in human form. Why? He came to show us that our coping mechanisms can't provide the healing and wholeness we want. He came to show those things for what they are: cheap substitutes for the Divine Love. These substitutes demand our attention, our adoration, and all the while, they drag us farther from the Divine Love. He came to cut us free of these cheap substitutes and to draw us into the Divine Love.

As Augustine said, Jesus became "human divinity and divine humanity." An audacious move. Even more audacious, Jesus didn't follow every jot and tittle of the religious leaders' law. He touched lepers in Divine Love, which was against the law. He ate with women of negotiable affections in Divine Love, which was at least against the social code. He turned his head the other way (in Divine Love) when his disciples picked a handful of grain on the Sabbath, a violation of the labor laws. And though Jesus flouted their made-up rules time and time again, his actions showed what he was all about. He didn't come to undermine the law—not specifically. He came to show us the divine policy of the law—love. What's more, he came to show us how to live into that love.

120. JESUS KNEW DESIRE

Jesus took on flesh and "dwelt among us," which is the Scriptures' highfalutin way of saying he came to eat and drink and fish and laugh and teach and be with us. In his fully divine humanity, he experienced the same pain, the same brain chemistry, the same temptations to elevate the created objects over the Creator we do. He knew the pull of the vices, the want of every damned desire. The writer of the letter to the Hebrews says just that: "For we do not have a high priest who is unable to empathize with our weaknesses, but we have one who has been tempted in every way, just as we are—yet he did not sin" (Heb. 4:15). Perfect God and perfect man, he came to show us the possibility of waking sobriety, of drawing our strength, our life from attachment to the Creator.

121. How Jesus Overcame Desire

As one who was "tempted in all things," Christ must have known just how easy it is to disorder our loves, to chase created things even over the Creator. He experienced the temptation of the bottle, of food, of sex, of shopping. He felt the temptation to elevate his ego, to ring the bell when he gave or forgave or healed. (Perhaps this is why he so often instructed the healed not to out him as the Messiah. See Mark 3:7–12; 5:40–43; Luke 8:51–56.) He must have felt the tug to torture his enemies. Time and time again, though, Jesus overcame these temptations, and not because he followed the letter of the law or some rule-keeping rubric. Instead, Jesus' strength flowed from his pure devotion and perfect attachment to the call of Divine Love.[2]

---

2 For an example of Christ's overcoming Old Scratch, read Matthew 4:1–11, where Jesus resists the twisting of the following pleasures: food, status, and wealth.

122. A DEEPER AWAKENING

After passing a devilish test, Jesus returned to the people, and he brought a new message. Standing on a mountainside, he delivered his most famous sermon to the masses—the religious leaders, tax collectors, zealots, somewhat religious workaday folks, and perhaps a Roman soldier or two. There, Jesus showed how the dos and do-nots of the religious rules can't rid us of the lesser loves that choke our hearts.

Consider his teaching on two of the most straightforward commandments: thou shalt not murder, and thou shalt not do it with someone who ain't your spouse. If living into Divine Love were as simple as following the rules, wouldn't he just have reiterated these laws? Jesus knew better, though. He knew we can live lives of technical perfection and not worship the Lord our God and serve him only. He knew refraining from killing our neighbor or bedding his wife (or killing our neighbor *and* bedding his wife, as David did in the Old Testament) doesn't mean we are loving both God and neighbor. Aren't the fantasy of punching your neighbor in the eye and actually punching him fueled by the same hate and anger? (Matt. 5:21–22). Isn't objectifying his wife in the hidden room of your imagination the antitheses of Divine Love? (Matt. 5:27–30).

See? Jesus knew that true sobriety—a sobriety characterized by living in the love of God—requires a deeper sort of awakening, an awakening to our underlying emotions, desires, imaginations, even our pain.

123. JESUS IN TIMES SQUARE

Being human divinity and divine humanity, Jesus also knew there are plenty of legal things we can use or misuse to numb the pains of life. Eating, drinking, shopping—there might be no commandment or rule against these things, but he knew the ways we can turn them into coping mechanisms. Consider his teaching in the Sermon on the Mount: "Do not be anxious about your life, what you will eat or what you will drink, nor about your body, what you will put on. Is not life more than food, and the body more than clothing? Look at the birds of the air: they neither sow nor reap nor gather into barns, and yet your heavenly Father feeds them. Are you not of more value than they?" (Matt. 6:25–26 ESV).

If we imagined Jesus in a modern context, if we dropped him into Times Square and gave him a bullhorn, he might say it to us this way: "Stop trying to eat, drink, and dress your way out of your worry. Doesn't your Father take care of those pigeons pecking around your feet? And the unpopular truth is this: he extends a deeper expression of love to you than he does those flying rats."

Doesn't it stand to reason that Jesus knew just how anxiety (pain) fuels our wardrobe fixations, our gluttony, our drunkenness? Still, he doesn't tell us to stop shopping, eating, or drinking. Instead, he teaches us to recognize the pain for what it is, and, instead of turning to acquisition to fix that pain, to turn in to God's love, Divine Love that provides for all of our needs (Phil. 4:19).

124. WARNING: THIS BIT ABOUT MONEY MIGHT PINCH A LITTLE

We use so many things to sooth our human anxieties, none more than money. And was there any commandment against making money back in the biblical age? Is there any prohibition on it now? Haven't humans from time immemorial celebrated the wealthy of the age?

Jesus knew how the human heart turns to money to silence the narratives of pain, particularly the narrative of scarcity. So he didn't hold back in his great sermon.

Money is an enticing lover, he said, one that begs for adoration.

It's impossible to adore two lovers, he said, God and money.

Eventually, one lover will demand full adoration, he said, and that lover will squeeze the other out.

And what happens when we turn our adoration, our gaze, to money thinking it will cure our ills? As if to drive the point home, Jesus drops this observation in the middle of his teaching on money: "The eye is the lamp of the body. So, if your eye is healthy, your whole body will be full of light, but if your eye is bad, your whole body will be full of darkness. If then the light in you is darkness, how great is the darkness!" (Matt. 6:22–23 ESV).

Though I've had this Scripture passage hung around my neck by well-meaning folks cautioning against the perils of *Playboy* or the sin of late-night Cinemax or the naked internet, that's not the point of Jesus' teaching. He means for us to examine a deeper lust, the kind that drags us down to dark sleep: money.

Money—it's a lover more false than those bouncing bodies.

Money—it's a temptation greater than skin on the screen.

Money—it's a serial betrayer.[3]

Washington, Jackson, and Franklin—if we fix our gaze on you, how dark will our gaze be?

---

3   Modern prophet the Notorious B.I.G. found these assumptions to ring true. After experiencing so much success, he said, "The more money you make, the more problems you get."

125. Allow Me to Keep Pinching: The Anxiety of the Affluentish

Money: the love of it works through our bodies like leaven, multiplying. It supplants our love for God in so many ways, even when we can't see it. And if you're reading this book, chances are you're affluent or at least affluentish. You might not feel affluent for any number of reasons: the insurance premiums have you by the throat; the credit card debt is pushing you to bankruptcy; you can't make the math work on your student loan payments; you might not have a pot to whizz in, and not because you're some eco-chic minimalist who runs a monochromatic home-design blog. But there's a difference between feeling affluent and actually being affluent.

Don't you live in a material society with access to enough material to get by?

Don't you have shelter? (I do.)

Food? (I do.)

A couple of sets of extra undies? (If you don't, email me. I'll send you a care package.)

Even though you have enough, maybe you're like me. Maybe you feel the insatiable want of more. More money. More material. More security. And if there's a possibility you could get more, then chances are you're affluentish.

So ask yourself whether you have some of the characteristics of the affluent, whether you're affluentish.[4] Do you believe that grabbing more than enough is possible? Do you fixate on the privileged possibility of having more than enough? This fixation spreads like leaven, like a virus. This fixation can drag us down to sleep.

---

4 Some websites indicate that the suffix *ish* carries connotations of fixation, focus, or addiction.

126. BACK TO JESUS

Jesus knew we could follow the right rules (thou shalt not kill; thou shalt not commit adultery) and still be attached to our desires (anger and lust). He knew we might chase socially acceptable vices in an effort to alleviate our anxieties—vices like food, drink, clothing, and money—and that those socially acceptable objects might drag us into the darkness. What's more, he knew we might attach ourselves to good and laudable things—like Proper Theology™, right living, and service to the poor—in an effort to satisfy our egos.[5]

"Why do you protest the sawdust in your brother's eye while ignoring the two-by-four in your own eye?" he asked (Matt. 7:3).

"Beware of being holy on Twitter in order to be retweeted," he said (Matt. 6:1).

"When you give to the needy, do not announce it with kazoos or bagpipes. Don't be a hypocrite and give to be honored by others," he said (Matt. 6:2).

You don't have to read between the lines. Jesus knew that even good theology, good works, and good giving can become coping mechanisms. Jesus knew that once mired in those good and laudable coping mechanisms, we'd lose sight of the Divine Love behind it all.

---

5   And as no small aside, if Jesus spoke against nursing *afección* for our egos and judgment, what would he think about the carnival of ego and judgment that's modern social media?

127. The Gifts of God

Jesus knew we'd attach to food, wine, clothing, money, giving, Proper Theology™, and a host of other things (including Twitter or video gaming or whatever). But still, he didn't come preaching against the objects of his creation, the Stuff of Earth. He knew that when we're rooted in the Divine Love of God first, we see these things for what they are: good gifts from a good God. In his discussion of food, drink, and clothing, he said, "Seek first his kingdom and his righteousness [attach first to God], and all these things [the Stuff of Earth] will be given to you as well" (Matt. 6:33). In the gospel of John, Jesus puts it this way: "I am the vine; you are the branches. . . . If you remain in [attach to] me and my words remain in you, ask whatever you wish, and it will be done for you" (John 15:5, 7).[6] See? The pleasures of earth aren't inherently evil. They can be great blessings when we use them as blessings of Divine Love. (See section 18, "The Implicit Rule of Human Being.") They can draw us even deeper into God's Divine Love.

---

6 This is not some Osteenian theological promise that if we abide in Christ we'll receive a Bentley, a private jet, and a fat load of cash. Attaching to Christ means attaching to his desires, his wishes, and in that, we find the things we want changed. Generally speaking, I agree with Biggie Smalls: "the more money you make, the more problems you get" (https://www.youtube.com/watch?v=gUhRKVIjJtw). That, of course, would be a different book, one someone has most certainly written. (For example, see *The New Demons* by Jacques Ellul.)

THE BOOK OF WAKING UP

128. Jesus' Relentless War against Disordered Affections

Time and time again Jesus addressed the coping mechanisms (the disordered attachments) of the people, the ways they were prone to adore the gifts instead of the Giver. Each time, he offered a similar solution, which can be summed up this way: "Wake up! Detach from the Stuff of Earth and attach yourselves to me!"[7] For the sake of argument, let's examine two such stories of attachment.

---

7   Rich Mullins, the late prophet-bard, wrote, "There's a loyalty that's deeper than mere sentiment, and a music higher than the songs that I can sing. The stuff of earth competes for the allegiance I owe only to the giver of all good things."

129. Attachment Story No. 1: Really? Money Again?

A wealthy, young, important, maybe even virile man came to Jesus, asked what he'd need to do to make the eternal guest list.

"Keep the commandments," Jesus said.

"I'm meticulous in my practices of purity," the fella said with a smile (which as you now know doesn't mean he necessarily kept the commandments).

"Great. Leave your fame and love me. Divest yourself of your fortune by giving it to the poor. Hitch your wagon to me and let's blow this dusty town."

The request—attach your affections to me—was too much, and the Scriptures record that the rich man went away sad. It was a master move on Jesus' part, one that showed how simply obeying all the laws (doing all the right things and abstaining from all the wrong things) doesn't produce attachment to the Divine Love.

130. ATTACHMENT STORY NO. 2: THE ONE ABOUT REAL BREAD

John—the mystic storyteller and beloved disciple of Jesus—tells a similar story, substituting a crowd for the rich young ruler and bread for material possessions. In John's story, we find Jesus face to face with a crowd of folks he'd fed by way of a miracle just a day earlier. (You recall the story of Jesus' feeding the five thousand with five small barley loaves and two little fish?) Jesus knew what they wanted: another miraculous meal, another free lunch, relief from the hunger pains. It's worth noting this crowd wasn't engaged in any illicit activity, and they were following Jesus. Still, their hearts (and appetites) were attached to something other than the Divine Love Jesus offered.

Confronting the crowd, Jesus gave them the hard truth. The previous day's bread was meant to point to a different sort of bread, a heavenly bread. He said, "*I am* the bread of life. Whoever comes to me will never go hungry, and whoever believes in me will never be thirsty" (John 6:35, emphasis added). And when the religious leaders grumbled against him for making this statement, he doubled down as if to remove any doubt. "*I am* the living bread that came down from heaven," he said. "Whoever eats this bread will live forever. This bread is my flesh, which I will give for the life of the world" (John 6:51, emphasis added).

What had been mild grumbling turned into a full-on argument, according to John, and that's when Jesus swung for the fences. "Very truly I tell you, unless you *eat the flesh* of the Son of Man and *drink his blood,* you have no life in you. Whoever *eats my flesh* and *drinks my blood* has eternal life, and I will raise them up at the last day. For my flesh is real food and my blood is real drink. Whoever eats my flesh and drinks my blood *remains in me*" (John 6:53–56, emphases added).

Loaves and fishes satisfy for a season. We take them in, break them down. Incorporate their nutrients into our bodies. In a very real sense, we attach their elements to ours. (More and more loaves seem to be attaching to my midsection as I age.) In a very real sense, bread becomes one with us. But Jesus knew that bread (or wine or fame or money or whatever) won't satisfy our Eden-born existential angst. So he offered a different sort of food and drink.

Eat my flesh.

Drink my blood.

Take *me* into your lives.

Incorporate all my elements—my body, my soul, my Divine Love—into your elements because I'm the only thing that will satisfy your hunger.

An audacious invitation.

An invitation to the most intimate attachment.

131. THE WAYS WE TURN BACK

What happened when the people heard this audacious invitation? The Scriptures record that "many of his disciples turned back and no longer followed him" (John 6:66). But this is not to say they didn't eat and drink other things, that they didn't incorporate something else into their bodies. (We all incorporate something into our bodies.) It is to say they turned from the holy invitation to true life and toward human liturgies of death, liturgies that went something like this:

> On the night they turned their backs to him, the people took food and work and money and sex and approval and entertainment and religious practice and whatever, and when they had given thanks to themselves for providing the food and work and money and sex and approval and entertainment and religious practice and whatever, they said, "Take, eat, use, get high: This is the Stuff of Earth, which is ours for the taking. Do this to kill the pain, at least for a night."[8]

---

8 The liturgy of life, as memorialized by the Book of Common Prayer, is markedly different: "On the night he was handed over to suffering and death, our Lord Jesus Christ took bread; and when he had given thanks to you, he broke it, and gave it to his disciples, and said, 'Take, eat: This is my Body, which is given for you. Do this for the remembrance of me.'"

132. JESUS USED BREAD TO POINT TO THE TRUE BREAD, WINE TO POINT TO TRUE WINE

Yes, Jesus came preaching a message of proper attachment: *Don't attach to the Stuff of Earth. Attach to me, the only one who can satisfy you.* But still, he used the Stuff of Earth to draw the people into that attachment. In the aforementioned gospel story, he used loaves and fishes to point to himself as the bread of heaven. In the water-to-wine miracle in Cana, he used wine to point to himself as the true life of every party.[9] He used water as an object lesson to invite a serial divorcee into his eternal love (John 4:7–15). He used spit and mud to give sight to a blind man (John 9:6). He even used a coin to invite the religious leaders out of fixation on the Roman Empire and into the eternal kingdom (Mark 12:16–17).

See? For Christ, all material is useful for drawing us into the Divine Love of God. He uses the Stuff of Earth to direct us to the love of heaven.

---

9   See section 25, "The Life of Christ Speaks of Sacramentality."

133. This Being the Case...

It should be no surprise that on the night he was betrayed—the world's darkest night—Jesus again used earthly matter to draw his disciples deeper into the mystery of attachment with the Divine Love (John 6:56). In an upstairs room somewhere in Jerusalem, Jesus shared the worst news: There was a traitor in their midst, one who'd set the dominoes falling, and by the same time on the following day, Jesus would be dead. Pain was coming to visit Christ, and this pain was the worst pain, the pain of all the world's sin (1 John 2:2). Though his disciples didn't understand it at the time, it was in the context of that pain that he instituted the meal meant as an eternal reminder that he came to satisfy our deepest hunger, the hunger for substantive love.

Breaking the bread at the table, he passed it to the disciples and said, "Take and eat; this is my body" (Matt. 26:26). After they ate, he took a cup of wine, and blessing it, he said, "Drink from it, all of you. This is my blood of the covenant, which is poured out for many for the forgiveness of sins" (vv. 27–28).

This bread is my flesh, the bread of life.

This wine is my blood, the wine of life.

Do this over and over again, for millennia upon millennia, until I come again.

Descendants of the disciples as we are, we still eat and drink those sacramental gifts made sacrament today, and that eating and drinking is a way of incorporating his elements, his life, into ours. These simple pleasures draw us into the eternal pleasure of his sacrificial love.

134. JESUS ATTACHED TO GOD IN THE PAIN

Had Jesus been nothing more than some crackpot pundit, he might have just spewed a few thousand words on the ways our desires lull us to sleep, on how important it is to attach ourselves to him and his Divine Love instead of to any material thing. He might have skipped the institution of the awkward Last Supper too. But God, in flesh as he was, chose a more representational path. After instituting the Last Supper, he walked headlong into the pain. As he did, he demonstrated the way of perfect attachment to the Divine Love. He demonstrated a perfect waking sobriety.

135. JESUS AND THE NARRATIVES OF PAIN

After Judas sold Jesus out for a fistful of silver (see how the love of money betrayed Judas's *afección*), Christ was seized, tried, convicted, and led to the cross. There, he was met with the pains of life, and he heard their narrative of pain too.

Scarcity: You're out of time, out of friends, out of breath.
Abuse: No one is safe, not the Romans who crucify you, the religious leaders who condemn you, the people who mock and spit on you.
Loss: Hasn't God left you to die alone?

Fully divine as he was, he could have created twelve jugs of wine and numbed the narratives of pain. He could have silenced the pain by conjuring a week's worth of narcotics or summoning a billion bucks to offer as a bribe or ordering up an army of sentient robots to annihilate his captors. He didn't do any of those things. Instead, he walked into the pain awake, rooted in the Divine Love.

How do we know?

We remember his dying words. All of them.

136. JESUS AND HIS ATTACHMENT TO THE FATHER

In the midst of the worst pain humans could dish out, Jesus showed us how to be attached to God, even when he must have been thirsting for some anesthetizing agent.

In the garden, he begged God, praying, "Father, if it is possible, may this cup be taken from me. Yet not as I will, but as you will." On the cross, he again pushed into the Divine Love of the Father, and instead of hating his murderers, he extended that Divine Love to them, praying, "Father, forgive them." At the end of his darkest hour, he invoked the Divine Love again, praying, "Father, into your hands I commit my spirit."

Jesus never once turned to the Stuff of Earth for relief from emotional pain. He didn't let hate or anger for his enemies limit his expression of love. He didn't once elevate the creation (even his created emotions) over the Creator either, didn't lash out at God or curse him. As he shouldered the weight of the world's brokenness, he kept his eyes fixed on the Divine Love of his Father, even allowing the pain to draw him deeper into that love.

137. THE WAKING POWER OF DIVINE LOVE

Jesus is the perfect example of attachment to the Divine Love, especially during pain, and three days after his death, Divine Love woke him from the grave, beating the hell out of death as he did (1 Cor. 15:57). Now we see the power of his Last Supper invitation: If we hitch our lives to his, if we incorporate his being into ours, we'll find ourselves pulled from the darkness of death by the pain slayer. And as we're drawn upward in unity to Christ, we'll experience Christ's ultimate promise: "Take heart! I have overcome the world" (John 16:33).

138. THIS IS DIVINE SOBRIETY

See? For Jesus it wasn't all about the rules, the dos and do-nots. He knew we could just say no to drugs, refrain from overdrinking, and put site blockers on our website browsers and still be asleep to God's love. All the rules in the world won't lead us into a life of divine sobriety. So the way I see it, the sobriety Jesus preached is marked by three characteristics:

1. Being so incorporated into the Divine Love of God that every created thing (bread, wine, even pain) draws us ever deeper into that love
2. Letting go of the created things we're prone to use as substitutes for the healing, resurrecting, life-giving, restoring Divine Love
3. Pushing into the Divine Love through eating his body, drinking his blood, walking as he walked, praying as he prayed, loving as he loved, blessing as he blessed

139. What Was Poison Can Become Healing

Living into this kind of sobriety—the kind that orders the love of God above all other things—we can do or not do a whole host of things. We can pick things up (like wine, money, and Twitter) or put them down. We can see all material, all creation, as an expression of God's grace to us and an invitation to participate more fully in his Divine Love. Rooted in this sobriety, we don't have to be afraid of the Stuff of Earth, because we know the whizz-bang of the Stuff of Earth becomes nothing more than a sorry substitute for divine *afección*. What's more, on occasion, the objects that once were our poison might become the means of our healing.[10]

That's a bold statement, you say.

It is. I lived it.

---

10 Granted, this is not to say that you can pick up heroin or porn or any of the destructive and often illegal things. There are some prohibitions worth keeping, and though I'll not list those here, I'll encourage you to employ common sense on the matter.

140. My Story of Drinking after I Stopped Drinking

We're sitting in the living room, the dregs of a good dinner party gracing the table. A leftover chunk of rustic bread. A plate of uneaten olives. A greasy plate emptied of cheese. A quarter bottle of undrunk red.

It'd be a shame to let the bread and wine go to waste, the minister in attendance says, pouring the wine into a water goblet. They laugh. I don't. He doesn't turn the glass up like I thought he might. Instead he takes it in his right hand, reaches for the bread with his left. He holds them up, recites the words of institution.

This is my body.

This is my blood.

Take, eat, drink, and whatnot.

Float above the table. Be a fly on the ceiling. Watch the group pass the objects of creation—flour, yeast, fermented grapes. See me wringing my hands, swaying side to side, eyes squeezed shut. Fly down to my empty dinner plate. See how shallow my breathing is? Scan the partygoers, see them staring at me, wearing a collective expression of fresh alarm as they remember a shaky six-months' sobriety. Had anyone thought through this whole cup-of-salvation thing? Would Christ's blood wash me off the wagon?

Mike sits to my left, and he takes a chunk of bread and dips it in the water goblet of wine. He eats, then passes the last bread chunk and wine goblet my way. Hold your breath with him, with the rest of the table, with me.

Is a sobriety that can't withstand communion any sobriety at all? Let's find out.

The bread is a sponge, and when I dip it into the wine, it fills fast. *Take. Eat. Remember.* In the eating, a portal opens. I know this smell, this flavor, don't I? The flavor of my skinned palm when I fell off my bike as a boy. The smell of the delivery room when my firstborn came screaming into life. The taste of the thumb I almost lost to a chef's knife a year ago. It's salt and iron, water and wound, flesh and blood. It's full-bodied.

What I'd once considered some sort of metaphorical memorial takes the form of a real presence in that moment—bread and wine full of life. The wine of my poison—it has become the substance of salvation.

141. "SOBRIETY" TRANSUBSTANTIATED

In a living room in Arkansas, the word *sobriety* changed in substance. It was the moment I thought about it less as rule keeping (to drink or not to drink) and more as a way to attach to the Christ who'd made himself known to me in the bread and wine. In the days that followed that experience, I sought to connect with that Divine Love again and again, and as I did, I discovered that all those rules about not drinking kept me focused on one thing—drinking. And all the focus on drinking had me missing the transfer addictions.

At the end of a stressful day, did I turn to prayer, or did I pour a bowl of cereal? Did I invite God into my stress, or did I one-click another book on Amazon? Did I turn to the adoration of God's Divine Love, did I incorporate his body into mine, or did I guilt Amber to bed early in an attempt to blow off a little stress? Was I awake to the Divine Love of God in my life, the love that wanted to unite me with his overcoming resurrection, or was I still medicating in other ways?

This connection with the Christ of the bread and wine marked the beginning of my search for true, inner, waking sobriety. A sobriety that is less about avoiding addiction and more about the practice of adoration. It is a way of seeing the Stuff of Earth with eyes wide open. A way of understanding how all things—bread, books, clothing, making money, and even wine—are divine portals to draw us deeper into his Divine Love.

142. THE POINT IN THE BOOK AT WHICH I HAVE A HYPOTHETICAL CONVERSATION WITH THE SELF-IDENTIFIED ALCOHOLICS

You: "Wait a second. Are you saying I can drink again if get my attachments in order?"

Me: "No, no, no. At least, not exactly."

You: "Um . . . thanks for clearing that up? What exactly are you saying, then?"

Me: "Know yourself, your limitations, the strength of your attachments. Don't touch the stuff you can't control, the stuff you'll adore and elevate over the Divine Love. Don't take a sip of the communion wine if the communion wine will lead you into relapse. But to drink or not to drink—that's not the point of sobriety."

You: "So what's the point?"

Me: "It's not so much a point as it is a question: Are you awake to the God who draws all waking people deeper into Divine Love?"

You: "I'm not sure. How do I wake to that love?"

Me: "Good question."

How Do We Wake to the Sober Way?

Here comes the sun, and I say, It's all right.

—The Beatles

143. WAKE INTO THE DIVINE LOVE

Jesus came with a bullhorn and a message: "Keep awake—for you do not know when the master of the house will come, in the evening, or at midnight, or at cockcrow, or at dawn, or else he might find you asleep when he comes suddenly. And what I say to you I say to all: Keep awake" (Mark 13:35–37 NRSV). How should we stay awake, though? We attach to Christ as he attached to his Father; we abide in him as he abides in the Divine Love of God.

This waking attachment—how do we make it a reality in our lives? I haven't figured it all out, of course, but in my journey, I've found a few truths. And at the risk of reductionism, I've come to see waking into a more holistic sobriety as involving three steps.

Step 1: Wake to your pain and invite God into it.

Step 2: Wake to your coping mechanisms, your lesser loves and confess them.

Step 3: Wake to the Divine Love and pursue it as best you can.

144. Step 1: Wake to the Pain (A Story)

I stood on the platform of a church in Megamidwest City, USA, sharing my journey of inner sobriety with a group of church leaders, pastors and lay leaders alike. I shared how I walked away from the bottle, woke to the pain of scarcity (of faith, healing, the whole shebang), and explored the reasons for my season of inebriation. I shared how all addictions are lesser loves, substitutionary gods, ways of seeking relief outside the healing power of God. Detaching from these lesser gods is possible, I said, but only if we're willing to reorder our attachments, only if we're willing to elevate the Creator over any object of creation.

I said my piece, maybe prayed a prayer, and I stepped from the stage. A line formed. Three. Then four. Ten. Person after person shared their story, each talking about their sneaky habits, their hidden addictions, how each of those addictions were born of some pain. The porn addict developed his habit trying to cope with the pain of sexual awakening in puberty, and that habit followed him into his later life, now threatening his on-the-rocks marriage. A preacher with an eating disorder (an Alex) shared of the chaos of his abusive home. Eating (or rather not eating) was the only thing he could control, and that attachment to control followed him through college until he sought therapy. Then came the cutter. Then the media junky. Then one with six pairs of fine-leather boots. They all shared how pain motivated their coping mechanisms.

Pain. Pain. Pain.

One of the conference attendees hung back, a younger man who hid his baby face with a patchwork beard. He was last in line. He'd made sure of it. The sanctuary clearing, he introduced himself, hands shaking, chin quaking. He was traveling with enough drugs to tranq a horse, he said. He'd taken three times the prescribed amount already, he said, and it was only 2:00. He was in a vortex. A dark spiral.

"The problem is, I don't really have any pain," he said, tears pooling at the corners of his eyes.

"The problem," I said, "is that you're blocking, avoiding, or lying about the pain."

He stood blinking, staring. I pushed more, asked about the first time he felt the kind of anxiety he experiences when he's coming down from his horse tranquilizers. The tide rose in his eyes and he couldn't hold it back. Two awkward minutes later, composure gained, he outed his secret. There'd been abuse. *That* kind of abuse. A few years. Many nights. Always a secret. Night after night as he put his head on his pillow, he wondered whether he'd wake to the abuse again, whether he'd be told to keep secrets again. And again. And again. The shame, the guilt, the pain—it soaked through him, pooled on the floor in front of me.

He finished sharing his story, then said something I hadn't expected.

"I don't understand. For twenty years I've said I forgave him. But still, every time I think of him, I come apart."

"Forgiveness isn't a silver bullet," I said.

"That's not what the seminary taught," he said.

"Did you ever tell them about the abuse?" I asked.

"I didn't see the need," he said.

"Have you talked with your church staff about your pill problem, about the abuse of your childhood?"

"No," he said. "I'm afraid they'll think I'm unfit for ministry or ask me to take time off. I'm afraid I won't be able to take care of my family," he said.

He wasn't the first minister to share how he'd pushed back the pain, hidden his coping mechanisms in an effort to keep his job. (He wasn't the last either.) But in the waking realization, he made an impromptu promise. He'd invite God into the pain and ask him to bring him peace. He'd talk with his supervisor, his elders, whoever needed to know, and he'd get real help.

Waking into sobriety—is it possible without pulling the blanket off our pain, without staring it down with fresh eyes, without exploring the nexus between it and our addictions, habits, and dependencies?

145. WHAT HAPPENS WHEN WE WAKE TO PAIN?

In a *Time* magazine article in 2015, Mandy Oaklander wrote about the pain-reducing properties of mindfulness meditation. Reviewing a study by Dr. Fadel Zeidan, professor of neurobiology and anatomy at Wake Forest Baptist Medical Center, Oaklander concluded that "past research indicated that opioid morphine reduces physical pain by 22 percent—and [meditation] has surpassed even that."[1] But it wasn't just the reduction in pain that was intriguing. Oaklander writes, "People who had practiced mindfulness meditation seemed to be using different brain regions than the other groups to reduce pain." The researcher found that the group using meditation "had increased activation in higher-order brain regions associated with attention control and enhanced cognitive control . . . while exhibiting a deactivation of the thalamus—a structure that acts as the gatekeeper for pain to enter the brain." It was a result not seen with any other pain-management mechanism.

Mindfulness meditation is fine and good, and I'm not here to knock it. (In fact, I find it useful.) But still, doesn't mindfulness meditation leave you feeling alone? Focused and prayerful meditation, inviting God to sit with you in the confession of your pain, imagining him tending to it—this is the stuff of divine connection.

In the days of my darkest pain, I sat in my living room chair every night and asked the God of comfort to come sit with me in my pain. In that chair, I contemplated the narratives of scarcity, how I hadn't had enough faith to be cured of asthma or to see my son cured. I considered the apparent absence of God. I shared my pain

---

1   Mandy Oaklander, "Meditation Reduces Emotional Pain by 44%: Study," *Time*, November 11, 2015, http://time.com/4108442/mindfulness-meditation-pain-management/.

in prayer with the God I questioned, and made meditative space
for him to work (or not). In the stillness and silence of that space,
releasing all expectations, here's what I found: the Healer of healers,
the Great Physician, began to soften the sting in his Divine Love.

146. Waking to Pain Requires Community

Waking to pain on one's own can be a dangerous proposition. The human experience is a minefield of memories, one that can be difficult to navigate alone. If the wartime analogy doesn't sound quite right to you, consider your human experience as an emotional ball of tangled yarn. It can be hard to pull the threads of your pain loose without an extra set of hands.

Thanks be to God, there is a qualified community of skilled people who are capable of walking with you through the darkness of your pain. We call these people therapists, and they have advanced degrees in navigating the minefield and detangling the human experience. (Consider this my encouragement to pick up the phone and give one a call. I don't suppose you'll be sorry.)

147. Step 2: Wake to Your Coping Mechanisms

"Know thyself"—it's a Greek maxim, one which was inscribed on the Temple of Apollo at Delphi. It's a maxim which appears with regularity in books written by modern-day self-help gurus, executive coaches, and counselors. It's used with such regularity that some might consider it cliche, and though I'm a fan of taking potshots at cliches, I'll let this one slide. I might even indicate that it's one of the most important extrascriptural maxims you might apply to your life.

Know thyself—what is it but a call to understand the pain of your life?

Know thyself—what is it but a call to examine the coping mechanisms you use to hold those pains at bay?

But how do you know whether your overshopping is an addiction, a coping mechanism? (After all, you haven't bankrupted your family, at least not yet.) How do you know if your use of social media is a coping mechanism? (Social media doesn't really get in the way of your work, at least not yet.) How do you know whether your drinking is a coping mechanism? (You don't get fall-down drunk, at least not yet.) Of course, I confess my inadequacy to answer these questions for others. (After all, I can't look into your soul.) So let me answer your questions this way: know thyself, thy coping mechanisms.

How?

Try a simple exercise.

148. THE KNOW-THY-COPING-MECHANISM EXERCISE

Find twenty minutes of stillness, solitude, and silence. Pen and journal ready, invite the presence of Divine Love into the moment and pray, "Look into my heart, my anxiety, my pain and see whether I'm attached to any coping mechanisms, any lesser loves. Wake me to those coping mechanisms, and lead me away from them and into your Divine Love." (See Ps. 139:23–24.) Then, sit. Wait. Pay attention to whatever coping mechanisms come to mind (and be ready, because they most certainly will) and write them down. Then, get curious and ask, "Do I use these to mute, numb, or distract myself from the pain narratives?"

149. Waking to Coping Mechanisms Might Require Community Too

You might wake to innocuous coping mechanisms—the Netflix binge, the incessant use of social media, the addiction to Candy Crush. Those things rob you of time, disrupt connection with God, but with a little confession, a little willpower, and a little accountability, can't you break those habits and addictions? (I think so.)

You may wake to darker coping mechanisms. Perhaps you're a sexaholic, a drug addict, or a problem drinker. There are some addictions that require a more proactive, stop-it-now-at-all-costs approach, an approach that will require the spiritual, emotional, and often physical support of community. You might need to check into rehab. Perhaps you should consider joining an AA or NA or SA group. Maybe a therapist will do.

When you wake to your coping mechanisms, surround yourself with a community of love, a community that invites confession. Out yourself, your coping mechanisms. Then stick close to that community of love, the community which will help you walk away from those disordered attachments and *afecciós*. If you don't, you might find yourself sliding back into the same old habits and addictions no matter how much self-will you assert.

Herein lies the great risk: if you fall asleep again, what if you never wake up?

150. Waking to Our Coping Mechanisms Is a Process

Waking to our coping mechanisms is not a one-time event, of course. It takes practice, examination. Saints throughout the centuries have known this, including St. Ignatius of Loyola, who asked us to be ever aware of our attachments. In the *Exercises*, he offers the First Principle and Foundation, which teaches us how our affections should be ordered to ensure we don't develop accidental coping mechanisms. Wordy as it is, I'll paraphrase it below, footnoting the complete text.

Paraphrase of St. Ignatius's First Principle and Foundation: You were created to be awake to God, to praise, love, and serve him alone. What is this but salvation? Everything else (bread, wine, sex, money, accomplishment) is made to help you praise, love, and serve God. So use those things as far as they help you praise, love, and serve God. If they don't? If they become coping mechanisms that distract you from attaching to him? Burn 'em. Trash 'em. Cut 'em off. Whatever. And to help you keep from creating new coping mechanisms, if an object of creation isn't illegal or immoral or doesn't flout the teachings of Jesus, be indifferent to those things so that they don't become coping mechanisms. Then you can pick the stuff up or put it down, depending on the season. But whatever you do, don't let anything distract you from your primary purpose: praising, loving, and serving God.[2]

---

2 "Man is created to praise, reverence, and serve God our Lord, and by this means to save his soul. The other things on the face of the earth are created for man to help him in attaining the end for which he is created. Hence, man is to make use of them insofar as they help him in the attainment of his end, and he must rid himself of them insofar as they prove a hindrance to him. Therefore, we must make ourselves indifferent to all created things, as far as we are allowed free choice and are not under any prohibition. Consequently, as far as we are concerned, we should not prefer health to sickness, riches to poverty, honor to dishonor, a long life to a short life. The same holds for all other things. Our one desire and choice should be what is more conducive to the end for which we are created."

151. Cutting Our Coping Mechanisms Loose

If, through examination, we discover coping mechanisms, created things we've elevated over the Creator, how do we detach from them and reorder our *afecciós* so the Divine Love embodied in Christ is our primary aim? St. Ignatius offers a master class on the topic in the *Exercises,* and though he offers various meditations and prayer practices throughout the *Exercises* that might be helpful in identifying and detaching from those coping mechanisms, I'll cherry-pick a few.

152. THE PRAYER OF OPPOSITES: A PRAYER TEMPLATE FOR ORDERING ATTACHMENTS

In *The Spiritual Exercises,* Ignatius examines the human propensity to attach to money, and he further examines how that attachment pulls us away from the light and love of God. He writes, "It should be noted that when we feel an attachment opposed to actual poverty or a repugnance to it, when we are not indifferent to poverty and riches, it will be very helpful in order to overcome the inordinate attachment, even though corrupt nature rebel against it, to beg our Lord [in prayer] to choose us to serve Him in actual poverty. We should insist that we desire it, beg for it, plead for it, of course, that it be for the service and praise of the Divine Goodness" (*Exercises*, 157).

Huh?

It's a jarring statement, especially for the affluentish. But St. Ignatius knew the narcotic effect of money, how it lulls us to sleep in the desert of death. And this being the case, he recommended a radical form of rehabilitation: pray for poverty.[3] And couldn't this prayer be applied to any number of addictions, habits, and coping mechanisms?

To overcome an inordinate attachment to sex, couldn't we ask the Lord to serve him in actual chastity?

To overcome an inordinate attachment to social media, couldn't we ask the Lord to serve him in analogue simplicity?

To overcome an inordinate attachment to people-pleasing or the praise of others, couldn't we ask the Lord to serve him in obscurity and anonymity?

Knowing how our coping mechanisms become attachments, we can turn to prayer, asking God to remove them and to grant us the grace of living in a condition of opposites so we might move deeper into the praise, love, and service of God.

---

3   This is a prayer I still haven't prayed. Perhaps this betrays a disordered attachment in my life?

153. Imagine Your Coping Mechanisms in the Hands of Jesus

Divesting prayers are efficacious, but some prayers are more imaginative, more embodied. In the *Exercises*, Ignatius recognizes that some foods and drinks might lead to addictions, drawing us away from attachment to Christ. (Aren't we a people who so often serve the God of our stomachs?) The saint writes, "As to drink, abstinence seems to be more necessary than in eating bread. Hence, one should consider carefully what would be helpful, and therefore to be permitted; and what would be harmful, and to be avoided. As to foods, greater and more complete abstinence is to be observed. For with regard to them the appetite tends more readily to be excessive, and temptation to be insistent" (*Exercises*, 211).

Like Jesus, Ignatius didn't prescribe abstinence from intoxicating drink or rich foods. Instead, he offered practical tips for bringing them under our attachment to Christ. We can make it our practice to drink ordinary drinks and eat ordinary ("coarser") foods. We can practice fasting too. But Ignatius didn't just offer practical advice for dealing with attachment to food and drink. He also offered a prayer practice rooted in the imagination, writing, "While one is eating, let him imagine he sees Christ our Lord and His disciples at the table, and consider how He eats and drinks, how He looks, and how He speaks, and then strive to imitate Him. In this way, his mind will be occupied principally with our Lord, and less with the provision for the body. Thus he will come to greater harmony and order in the way he ought to conduct himself" (*Exercises*, 214).

See how this prayer of imagination keeps Christ at the forefront of our minds? See how it's meant to keep us attached to his way of being instead of to food?

This imaginative prayer practice isn't just applicable to eating and drinking, though. In any temptation toward any coping mechanism, can't we imagine Christ and his disciples with us? Wouldn't that influence our actions?

When you're pulled to Cyber Monday sales, imagine Christ and his disciples sitting at the computer with you. How would they shop? Always in moderation, always as a means of partnering with God in meeting our physical needs or bringing joy to others?

When the issue *du jour* begs for online discussion, ask, "How would Christ and his disciples use social media?" Who knows, but one stretches to imagine a Christ who'd prioritize snarky digital banter over proximal healing connection.

When the narcotic needs come calling, imagine Christ and his disciples at the street corner, talking with a dealer. How would they take their heroin? Their unprescribed opioids? If I had my guess, I'd say not at all.

See how imaginative prayer holds all created things in Jesus' light? See how it helps us reorient the ways we eat, drink, spend, have sex, work, tweet, and play video games? See how it invites the Divine Love into every facet of our lives?

154. Step 3: Wake to the Divine Love

Having awakened to your pain and invited Christ in, having awakened to your coping mechanisms and begun the process of detaching from them, it's time to wake into the Divine Love of God and attach to it.

In his letter to the church at Ephesus, Paul invited the people to walk in the love of God, laying their lesser loves aside (idolatry, he called their coping mechanisms; Eph. 5:1–4).[4] Those coping mechanisms, he implied, pull us into the darkness, and so he gave a clarion call:

> "Wake up, sleeper,
>   rise from the dead,
>   and Christ will shine on you."

> Be very careful, then, how you live—not as unwise but as wise, making the most of every opportunity, because the days are evil. Therefore do not be foolish, but understand what the Lord's will is. Do not get drunk on wine, which leads to debauchery. Instead, be filled with the Spirit.
>
> —Ephesians 5:14–18

Substituting the light of Divine Love for the darkness of our coping mechanisms—could anything be more foolish? Yet when we wake to our coping mechanisms and walk from them, we wake into the light of Divine Love.

---

4   The text of Ephesians 5:3–4 reads, "But among you there must not be even a hint of sexual immorality, or of any kind of impurity, or of greed, because these are improper for God's holy people. Nor should there be obscenity, foolish talk or coarse joking, which are out of place, but rather thanksgiving."

155. WE, THE CHILDREN OF THE LIGHT

Paul pulled the same thread again in his letter to a band of believers in the Roman Empire, encouraging them to walk in the waking daylight of God's love instead of the darkness of debauchery (also known as our coping mechanisms). He writes, "You are all *children of light and children of the day; we are not of the night or of darkness. So then let us not fall asleep as others do, but let us keep awake and be sober;* for those who sleep sleep at night, and those who are drunk get drunk at night. *But since we belong to the day, let us be sober,* and put on the breastplate of faith and love, and for a helmet the hope of salvation" (1 Thess. 5:5–8 NRSV, emphases added).

See? In Paul's own *Book of Waking Up,* he reminds us that we are children of light, and what are children if not loved? He reminds us too of the very thing that protects our waking sobriety: the breastplate of Divine Love.

156. The Waking Community

Attaching to Divine Love, remaining awake in God's light, can be difficult, especially when those old coping mechanisms come calling. But there's good news. God didn't leave us to work this out alone. Just as we might need therapists to help us wake to our pain, just as we might need communities of care like AA or NA to wake from our coping mechanisms, God knew we'd need a community of faith to keep us awake.

Jesus came, perfect as he was, and even he shared his love in community. He gathered with disciples—men and women alike—and he ate with them, laughed with them, taught them. He invited them to incorporate his life into theirs through sharing a family meal around a Passover table in an upper room. After his resurrection, he showed the resurrection power of his Divine Love by appearing to that same community at the same family table. He'd later give them perfect union with him through the gift of the Holy Spirit (the Spirit of love and comfort), a gift given as they gathered in community in that same room.

In his love, Jesus gathered a community and called it his family, the church, the waking community. He shared the gifts of God (laughter, love, bread, wine, body, blood, his Spirit) with the people of God in that waking community. Through his Spirit, he continues to share those gifts with the waking community today.

So if you find difficulty experiencing the love of God, ask yourself, "Am I in a waking community?" And just because the sign out front says "church," it's not necessarily what Christ intended. Is there love in the air? Is there support as you reckon with your pain, as you come clean with your coping mechanisms? Do they serve the waking meal with some regularity, the meal of divine attachment?

"The waking meal?" you ask.

Ah, yes. The waking meal.

157. THE MEAL OF WAKING

In the community of waking, we gather to break bread and drink wine, but this is no ordinary bread and wine. That bread—Christ's flesh—and that wine—Christ's blood—are meant to pull us farther away from the Stuff of Earth and further into the Divine Love of Christ. They're meant as a reminder: we were made to ingest, incorporate, and take Christ's life into our own, and through that taking in, we nourish our attachment. How do I know? Jesus made the claim himself, saying, "Whoever eats my flesh and drinks my blood remains in [or attaches to] me, and I in [and to] them" (John 6:56).

In his letter to the fledgling faithful in Greece, Paul shares how the bread and the wine (sacramental objects) are meant to draw us from the desire of our coping mechanisms and into the Divine Love of Christ. Issuing a wakeup call to the church at Corinth—who were overindulging in food and drink, distracted with play, and prostrating themselves to sex—Paul writes, "Therefore, my beloved, flee from idolatry [aka, addiction and attachment to food, drink, sex, and play]. I speak as to sensible people; judge for yourselves what I say. The cup of blessing that we bless, is it not a participation in the blood of Christ? The bread that we break, is it not a participation in the body of Christ?" (1 Cor. 10:14–16 ESV).

In his Divine Love, Christ gave his body and blood as a sacrifice "for the forgiveness of sins" (his words, not mine), so that we could be righteous (Paul's words, not mine). So participating in the waking meal, the meal of his body and blood, should draw us away from our disordered coping mechanisms and pull us deeper into Divine Love. Shouldn't it?

In the waking community, we've been given the meal of waking, a meal made of material means—bread and wine. Through those tangible, material, sacramental means made sacrament, we're drawn deeper into participation with the body and blood of Christ, who promised, "Whoever eats my flesh and drinks my blood *remains in me, and I in them*" (John 6:56, emphasis added). This intimate connection, this remaining in, is the reason we call the waking meal communion. In it, we attach to and commune with the Divine Love.

158. THE WAKING SONGS

The waking meal draws us into deeper attachment with the Divine Love. (I might argue it's the primary mechanism he uses in the community of the church.) That's not the only way the waking community encourages us toward true, waking sobriety. In his letter to the Ephesians, Paul links waking sobriety to the songs of the community. After ringing the alarm and asking the people to "wake up, sleeper [and] rise from the dead," he writes, "Do not get drunk on wine, which leads to debauchery. Instead, be filled with the Spirit, speaking to one another with psalms, hymns, and songs from the Spirit" (Eph. 5:18–19).

It's an odd passage, one of the oddest in all of the Scriptures, if you ask me. If applied literally, consider the implications: The urge to reach for the bottle (or the fun-sized Snickers or the computer or the credit card) strikes. The biology of desire spins up and the old coping mechanisms come calling. The brain burns hot, maybe too hot. What to do? In an attempt to quell the temptation, you run to your neighbor's house, a friend from your community of faith, and ring the doorbell. When she answers, you launch into a rousing rendition of "God of Earth and Outer Space."

Literal interpretations miss the meaning, though. There's no magic in a hymn, and what's more, I don't think the hymns and songs are the point of Paul's writings. What is the point? Perhaps Paul's juxtaposition of addiction with "speaking to one another" gets to the heart of the matter. Maybe he is encouraging us to avoid the error of isolation and instead to push into communities connected to the Divine Love.

159. Participating in the Waking Community

The waking community—what is it but a shot of caffeine, a jolt of electricity, a pinch in the night? Perhaps it keeps us aware of the coping mechanisms that threaten to drag us down to sleep.

What else is the waking community? Maybe it's a hook God uses to draw us away from our lesser loves and into his Divine Love. (Could this be why Christ promised his community they'd become fishers of men?) Maybe it's a life preserver, one we can hold onto when our desires threaten to pull us back down to the deeps. Maybe it's a rope of encouragement, one which tethers us to the Divine Love of God when the pain comes calling. A New Testament writer says as much, writing, "Draw nearer and nearer to God with a clean heart and with confidence that you're free from guilt and accepted. Hold tight to the rope of hope; the love of God is faithful. And think up ways to pull others into the practice of Divine Love (and the good deeds that result), not giving up on the community (ahem . . . the church), as some do. Encourage, encourage, encourage each other to stick with it, because pain will come calling."

This is my paraphrase of Hebrews 10:22–25.[5] See how God, in his Divine Love, gave us a community which draws us into him? See how he gave us a community of encouragement, one which helps us stay attached?

---

5 "Let us draw near to God with a sincere heart and with the full assurance that faith brings, having our hearts sprinkled to cleanse us from a guilty conscience and having our bodies washed with pure water. Let us hold unswervingly to the hope we profess, for he who promised is faithful. And let us consider how we may spur one another on toward love and good deeds, not giving up meeting together, as some are in the habit of doing, but encouraging one another—and all the more as you see the Day approaching" (Heb. 10:22–25).

160. The Waking Practices

If there's one thing that's certain, it's that our desires will rear their ugly heads. Coping mechanisms will come calling at the most inopportune times, and what if that call comes when we're away on business or on vacation or shipwrecked on a deserted island stocked with aged rum? What if the temptation comes when we don't have access to the waking community, the waking meal, the waking songs? How do we stay sober then?

In the earliest evening of my sobriety, the days when any whiff of stress sent me hankering for a gallon of whiskey or a gin-and-tonic fountain, I often turned to personal waking practices. I'd steep tea and meditate. I'd sit in the silence. I'd invite God into the stress.

God, be with me in the pain of my son's sickness.

God, be with me in the stress, in the multiplying medical bills, in the sickening dollar signs settling in my stomach.

God be with me in the anxiety of needing to be more so I can produce more so I can pay more.

God, be with me in this cocktail of emotions that pulls me to the bottle.

A Scripture passage might come to mind during those unsettling prayers, and I'd reach for the Good Book, open, read, and imagine myself in the biblical narrative.

Night after night, these waking practices became my personal rhythms, my personal devotion. And as I sank into weeks and months of these practices, I found a curious thing. The God I questioned showed up.

We can devote ourselves to our coping mechanisms, or to the waking practices of silence, meditation, prayer, devotional reading. The saints knew this well. Consider the writings of sixteenth-century Jesuit St. Francis de Sales: "In short, devotion is simply a spiritual activity and liveliness by means of which Divine Love works in us, and causes us to work briskly and lovingly; and just as charity leads us to a general practice of all God's Commandments, so devotion leads us to practice them readily and diligently."[6]

What St. Francis de Sales calls "devotion," I call the waking practices, but no matter what you call them, his truth is just as true today. As I walked in wobbly kneed devotion, something approximating sobriety set in. Something approximating changed tastes. Something like a deep need to adore the Giver instead of the gin.

---

6   As of the writing of this book, the full text of St. Francis de Sales' *Introduction to the Devout Life* can be found at https://www.catholicspiritualdirection.org/devoutlife.pdf.

161. How Divine Love Answers Pain

In the waking community, eating the waking meal, singing the waking songs, and walking in the waking practices, we come to be more and more connected to the Divine Love. But how does that Divine Love answer our pain?

Good question.

Remember the narratives of pain from section 48? Even when you're most awake, you'll still hear them. But awake to the love of God, walking in it, practicing it, you'll hear the counternarratives of true sobriety too.

- Scarcity whispers, "There's never enough."
  Divine Love answers, "There's more than enough life-giving pleasure."
- Abuse pounds, "No one is safe."
  Divine Love answers, "No one can beat my love out of you."
- Loss reminds us, "You're always alone."
  Divine Love answers, "I am with you always, even to the end of the age."

These answers won't come overnight. They may take weeks, months, years. There's no quick fix to pain, no easy way to leave your lesser lovers. You can't snap your fingers and wake from the deep sleep that's sometimes so comfortable. The way of sobriety, the waking way, is a way of faith, and what is faith but the hope of a promise yet to be experienced?

Wake to your pain. Wake to your coping mechanisms. Wake to the Divine Love, as best as you can with whatever faith you have in this present moment. If you do, you'll begin waking to the most beautiful song. Keep waking and waking and waking and the tune will grow louder, come with more clarity. Days will pass. Weeks.

Months. And as you string those months together, the song of Divine Love will become more and more clear:

> Good morning to you. Good morning to you.
> This is the way we start a new day.

You'll learn to sing along with the song, and as you do, you'll find the truth of Jesus' words: "Come sing with me all you tired, groggy, sleepy, and heavyhearted folks. As you wake into my love, find real rest" (Matt. 11:28, my paraphrase). At least, this was my experience.

162. How Waking Gives Way to Waking

When the light shattered across the dim Methodist foyer in September 2013, its shards cut me somehow, woke me from a dead-drunk sleep. Two weeks later, still shaking steady, I was sipping tea and playing guitar when I noticed the most delicate flavors, which I recorded in my journal this way: "White tea. Hint of strawberry? Is that some orange peel? Rose hips. Honey." How were there so many flavors?

Waking gives way to waking, even the waking of taste buds.

As I bathed in those flavors, the strings on my guitar almost played themselves, my fingers traveling the neck with clean fluidity. How was there so much music locked in me? Where had it been all these years?

Waking gives way to waking, even the waking of passions.

The dry days set in, the days of sharper focus—mental, spiritual, dextral. But still there were harder awakenings to be had. I woke into more pain, into the realization that I was being haunted by the ghost of scarcity: *You didn't have enough faith to muster your own healing. You don't have enough faith to muster your son's. You've never had enough.* I woke into the realization that the only way to silence those pain narratives was to invite God into the moment. I woke to the truth that his Divine Love (how was there so much love?) was pulling me from my pit. I woke to the notion that he wanted to bring healing to me, to those in the world around me, to the very world itself.

Waking gives way to waking, even the waking to healing.

I woke even more, realized there were pain bearers in my past, people I needed to forgive. Like that slick-suited faith healer who smelled of revival sweat and Old Spice? Yes. Like myriad other people I'll never name on the page? Yes. And in that awakening, I realized how many people I'd hurt over the years, how my patterns of behavior had wrought pain in the lives of others.

Waking gives way to waking, even the waking of the need to forgive, to ask for forgiveness.

I woke and woke and woke, and all those awakenings led me to that living room miracle, the place where I met Christ in the breaking of the bread. There, I found the God who uses ordinary, material pleasures to draw us into more perfect *afecciòns*. There, I found how wine, the pleasure that'd once been my poison, could become a sacramental means of participation in the Divine Love of Christ. What a glad and happy irony. It's that happy irony that's been pulling me deeper into the experience of love all these years later.

Waking gives way to waking, which gives way to waking, which gives way to waking. And if I were a compulsive gambler, I'd drop a twenty spot on this bet: I'm not finished waking yet.

163. One Last Invitation

Maybe you're in need of a good waking. Perhaps you're growing uneasy in the drowsy intoxication of your coping mechanisms, your habits, addictions, and dependencies. Hear the song: *Good morning to you. Good morning to you.* Let it pull you from your drifting dreams and into the morning light of love. And as you wake from those years of sleep, hear the words of Divine Love: *Rise, let us go from here.*